Born
To
Manifest

Law of Attraction
Tools and Techniques

By Thomas Michael Murasso

Thomas Michael Murasso Enterprises

Clemmons, NC

Contact information:

Thomas Michael Murasso Enterprises

4140 Clemmons Road, Suite 218

Clemmons, NC 27012

(509) 471-7303

Email: info@borntomanifest.com

Web Site: www.BornToManifest.com

An application to register this book for cataloging has been submitted to the Library of Congress.

ISBN: 978-1-4303-2236-8

Printed in the United States of America

To anyone with the desire to know, to everyone who vibrates with this, to each one of us, and to the One in each of us, I dedicate this work to you.

It is my desire to give you a gift I was given so you may give it to others. I want to help you remember who and what you are, and to remember how powerful you are.

How will you remember? You will know by how you *feel*.

Our deepest fear is not that we are inadequate. Our deepest fear is that we are powerful beyond measure. It is our light, not our darkness, that most frightens us. We ask ourselves, who am I to be brilliant, gorgeous, talented and fabulous? Actually, who are you not to be?

You are a child of God. Your playing small doesn't serve the world. There is nothing enlightened about shrinking, so that other people won't feel insecure around you. We are born to make manifest the glory of God that is within us.

It's not just in some of us; it's in everyone. And as we let our own light shine, we unconsciously give other people permission to do the same. As we are liberated from our own fear, our presence automatically liberates others.

Nelson Mandela
1994 Inaugural Speech

Gratitude

Thank you, God, for being with me always. I love you.

Thank you, Mom and Dad. I love you for giving me life.

Thank you to my wife, Glaucia, for understanding and giving me precious time to write this book. I love you and I'm grateful to have you with me.

Thank you, Rhonda Byrne, the producer of the film, The Secret. I'm grateful for your gift.

Thank you, Esther Hicks for Abraham's philosophy and "scientific spirituality."

Thank you, Michael Losier, for giving me the confidence to train people in the Law of Attraction.

Thank you, Barry Goss, creator of Manifest Life, and the mentors he's gathered that have shown me different paths.

Thank you, Joe Vitale, Jack Canfield, Michael Beckwith, Bob Proctor, James Ray, Randy Gage, Dr. Robert Anthony, Michael Talbot, Debbie Ford, Ghalil, Gary Craig, Bob Scheinfeld, Carol Look, Vania Aquino de Souza, Me, and so many others who have guided me on my journey. I love you all.

It's not your work to make anything happen. It's your work to dream it, and let it happen. Law of Attraction will make it happen. In your joy, you create something, and then you maintain your vibrational harmony with it, and the Universe must find a way to bring it about. That's the promise of Law of Attraction.

Excerpted from a workshop in Larkspur, CA on 8/16/1998

Introduction and a Promise

Something attracted you here. You'll soon learn what that something is. I promise you, your exposure to this information will change your life.

You will learn the key to attracting the things you want in your life and how it works. You can experience change very quickly if you apply and do the work. You can start using this information immediately.

Are you excited about that?

I want you to promise me something. I want you to promise me that you're going to participate fully.

Maybe you like to jump around and skip chapters that you don't think will apply to you. Start at the beginning. Read and re-read until the end. You'll be utilizing the information you learn throughout the whole book starting with the first chapter. Underline or highlight parts you deem important. You'll need a journal to transfer thoughts, insights, notes and feelings. Your journal will also be your workbook.

I promise you that if you participate fully, you'll integrate this information and receive one of the greatest gifts given to mankind. Information that was almost lost, until now!

Are you excited about that?

People are where they are because that's exactly where they really want to be whether they'll admit that or not.

Table of Contents

This book is a compilation of ideas, information and teachings I've *attracted* from various sources including Michael Losier (lawofattractionbook.com), Barry Goss (manifestlife.com), Esther Hicks (abraham-hicks.com), The Secret movie (thesecret.tv), Joe Vitale (mrfire.com), James Ray (jamesray.com), Bob Proctor (bobproctor.com), Dr. Robert Anthony (drrobertanthony.com), Rosicrucian philosophy (rosicrucian.org), and the works of Wallace D. Wattles, Charles F. Haanel, and Edgar Cayce. As Michael Losier says, "There's only one way to teach this!" I trust I've assembled the information in an easily understood way so you can learn the tools and techniques to deliberately manifest abundance in all areas of your life.

Tom Murasso, March 5, 2007

I'd like to share my journey with you. I won't be taking you back to the very beginning of my journey, just this leg of it. Looking back, this part of my journey started with an auction I won on eBay.

I had gotten interested in Foreign Exchange trading, known as 4x, and was looking for information and 4x reports on eBay. I came upon an auction that included three eBooks for 99¢ and thought this was certainly within my *limited* budget (more on that word later) and won the auction.

The eBook on 4x was very informative; however, one of the other eBooks I received called *Manifesting Mindset* was mind-blowing! The more I read of this wonderful little eBook, the more the information felt right. It was almost as if I was *resonating* (another word we'll explore later) with what I was reading at a very deep soul level.

Here was a simple report on attracting every thing you wanted into your life, be it wealth, health, relationships, happiness, cars, houses, and whatever you desired, using a simple technique called *Deliberate Manifesting*. I didn't say it was easy, just simple! One of the reasons I'm writing this book is to make manifesting simple and easy!

Like most people, I've always had a struggle with money or should I say cash-flow. I always seemed to be able to get money, and always seemed to see it *flow* through my fingers paying for bills, things I wanted, and day-to-day living expenses. Consequently, I was always looking for new ways to make more money and 4x looked like a possible means to do so. However, this new word, *manifesting*, started to become an obsession with me. I couldn't get my hands on enough information about it. I began searching for more articles and anything else I could find. I wanted to learn and absorb all I could about manifesting.

Dr. Robert Anthony (www.drrobertanthony.com) was mentioned in the eBook. I had never heard of the man and I searched his name on the Internet and found several *free* (I like that word) articles written by him. Upon reading the information, I found Dr. Anthony was not your typical motivational guru. Here was a man speaking about having everything you want in life by using the power of your *thoughts*!

My eyes lit up. I felt a warm glow inside. I've been interested in metaphysical things from a very young age. Ever since I can remember I was asking myself the question, a question you may have asked yourself; "Why are we here? What is the purpose of life?"

I've come to realize the old saying "When the student is ready, the teacher will appear" was true. When I was younger I had no idea how to find the answer to my questions, but out of nowhere a book would come into my life, or I'd interact with someone new who would share something I'd consider a revelation of some sort.

I studied religions, theology, astrology, Carlos Castaneda, Edgar Cayce, numerology, tarot, Rosicrucian philosophy, palm reading, hypnosis, channeling; you name it, I thought I'd find an answer here or over there. But I'm getting side-tracked. Let me get back to my story.

After reading several articles by Dr. Anthony and several other manifesting authors, it happened. It was somehow *attracted* to me (more on that later). I really can't remember if it was a report I read, an email I received or what, but I found myself at a website called "The Secret" – (www.theSecret.tv) and right there was a link to a DVD they sold called of all things, ***The Secret***.

Now, I sure live up to my name as a doubting Thomas, but I was almost guided by an unknown force to click on the link, spend the $30.00 that I didn't have, and buy the movie. It arrived at my home a few days later and my wife and I watched ***The Secret*** movie. We were spellbound.

When it was over I was overcome with emotions. Unbelievable, amazing, oh my God, wow, shock, awe, tears, joy, shivers… all these emotions flooding through me. I remember saying to my wife, "I just received the greatest gift I ever received in my life!"

Stop reading here and go to the website and buy the DVD or watch the movie online. Come back after you pick your jaw up off the floor and I'll show you how I've come to understand the ***Secret***.

It's really not a secret. The secret is the ***Law of Attraction***, but most people have never been told about it. It's a

Universal Law, like the law of gravity and is always operating in our lives whether we know about the law or not.

We're born and our parents teach us what they have been taught and experienced, and society teaches us what it knows and **believes** (another word we'll talk about later). Then there are our school teachers, our preachers, TV, movies, people we look up to, etc. All these people and all these things have created our belief system of how reality *is* and more than likely that belief system talks a lot about fear, lack and limitation.

What a mess! Look around you. The world is a terrible place. There's poverty, hunger, disasters, and war. There's not enough oil, money, food, water, air, to go around. Only the rich can enjoy whatever they want and they're usually a cunning lot. I've heard rich people are self-serving, ego-driven and maybe even evil. They certainly aren't very spiritual or honest.

Life is a struggle. You wake up every day to face a lousy job with lousy pay. You work long hours and never have time for yourself, much less your spouse and family. Any relationship we have with God or spirituality takes place on the weekend and the harsh realities of life take up all of the rest of our time.

We watch TV and try to relax; anything to get our mind off of this muck. We listen and see how we're not as beautiful as the movie stars and how we don't have the money for the lifestyle they have. The commercials tell us what kind of pill we need to take for a symptom we never realized existed. We need to have insurance because we need to be prepared for the worst. We have to watch what we eat because it will make us fat or give us pimples or God forbid; mad cow disease! We hear that the bird flu is coming, the terrorist are at the airport, an asteroid is headed toward the earth, the ice caps are melting, the ozone layer is disappearing... damn, we're screwed!

Did anyone buy into that? How does it make you feel?

How about the TV news and the newspapers? There was a rape, a murder, the cost of food and gas is rising. Real estate prices are sky-high, I mean low, no I mean high...

The tabloids tell us so and so is such and such and has this and that and we don't, never have and never will.

Well I feel terrible just writing about this and here you are reading these words thinking, "Why did you have to remind me?"

Look at it this way. My tongue-in-cheek illustration above is really a good way to know what we *don't* want and my friends; I'll show you how I learned to use the *Law of Attraction* to get what you do.

Why do some people have what they want and most people have what they don't want? It's called the *Law of Attraction* and it's all about vibrations and energy!

Whatever we plant in our subconscious mind and nourish with repetition and emotion will one day become a reality.

Chapter One

The Universal Law of Attraction

Be careful what you wish for… you just might get it!

Did you ever hear that statement? Did you ever want something so bad; you felt the passion of that wish to the very fiber of your being?

Well, I'm here to tell you that you *do* get what you wish for. Even if your wish is that you *don't* want something. "Gee, I wish I didn't have so many bills!"

I'm sure you have heard expressions like; be careful what you wish for, it's karma, just my luck, what a coincidence, serendipity, kismet, it's what fate has in store for me, God's will, and many other words or statements that describe people, things and events that affect our lives seemingly beyond our control.

The words and expressions people use are another way of describing a scientific process in action, a universal law called the *Law of Attraction*.

Like the law of gravity, the *Law of Attraction* has been with us since the beginning of time and is always operating whether we realize it or not.

The *Law of Attraction* simply states: I attract into my life whatever I give my attention, energy and focus to... whether good… or bad!

It's all about *frequencies* and *vibrations*.

Have you ever gone into a store or a building and said, "Wow, the vibes are really good in here?" Or you meet someone and you think, "Gee, are they ever giving off a negative vibe?" Don't most people have similar experiences? We're describing a *feeling* we're having when we use the word *vibe*.

A vibe is something you feel. A vibe equals a mood or a feeling. The short 1960's hippy word *vibe* really comes from the longer word, *vibration*; a vibrational frequency.

The *Law of Attraction* is working with vibrations. We're talking about vibrational energy. In the vibrational world there are only *two* kinds of vibrations, and the two kinds of vibrational energy are *negative* and *positive*. Think of a magnet's attraction properties.

> *Your world is a living expression of how you are using and have used your mind.*

Vibrational Energy

Some words or moods that describe *negative* vibrational energy would include: *fear, anger, sadness, depression, frustration, guilt, jealously, envy* and many others.

A list of *positive* moods or feelings would include among others: *happiness, joy, excitement, love, passion, abundance, humor, compassion, accomplishment,* etc.

Your feelings and moods cause a vibration. The way you *feel* is the vibe you give off or send out. When you feel bad, you feel lousy, and you can almost feel a black cloud hanging over your head. You're giving off a *negative* vibration.

On the other hand, when you're feeling happy, you're giving off a high *positive* vibration and other people can feel it too. You've heard the expression, a smile is contagious. It is! When you're feeling good and sending out that positive vibration, most people will feel good just being around you. Your positive vibration makes them feel positive vibrations.

If you looked in a dictionary, every word in it that described a mood or feeling would fall into either the negative or positive vibrational category.

When do we have a mood or feeling? Always, and right now, and right now, and right now. Right now, we all have a mood or feeling. At every moment we are having a mood or a feeling that gives off a negative or positive vibe or vibration.

The *Law of Attraction* is a science. Its job is to **match** the vibration that it finds and to **respond** to that vibration.

Negative Nancy and Positive Pete

Negative Nancy wakes up first thing in the morning just a little bit cranky. Nancy is sending out a *negative* vibration and given what you've just learned, the *Law of Attraction* is finding that negative vibration and matching it.

As the *Law of Attraction* is matching Nancy's negative vibration, she gets up out of bed and she stubs her toe, and then she burns her toast and spills her coffee. Suddenly she can't find her keys and when she finally does, she has trouble starting the car. On the way to work, the traffic gets worse and she almost has an accident, and then when she finally arrives she can't find a parking spot and now that she's completely frazzled and frustrated Nancy's thinking, "I should have stayed in bed!"

Now you're starting to understand why Nancy's day got worse and worse and worse. It's because the *Law of Attraction* was checking and matching her negative vibration. It was checking and matching, checking and matching. Nancy was attracting the very negative energy she was sending.

The *Law of Attraction* was checking and matching Nancy's vibration, and as she was experiencing something negative, the *Law of Attraction* was checking and matching. As she continued to experience something negative, her vibration stayed the same and the *Law of Attraction* was checking and matching. Then she continued to experience something negative, her vibration stayed negative, and the *Law of Attraction* checked and matched. This turned out to be a never ending cycle of negativity.

Our friend, Positive Pete, got all excited about this client he attracted first thing Monday morning. It was the largest sale that he'd had since he started with his company. Pete was so pumped up about that client. He called ten of his friends to brag about it saying, "Wow! I've got the best client ever!"

While Pete was celebrating and bragging about that ideal client, he was sending out a *positive* vibration and the *Law of Attraction* was checking and matching. He was really feeling great. A couple of hours later he gets more great clients and more big sales and says, "Wow, am I ever on a roll!"

Understanding the Law of Attraction

The *Law of Attraction* has been with us since the beginning of time. It is the law that regulates the order of the universe, the order of your life, and all of our experiences. No matter who you are or where you live, the *Law of Attraction* is always responding to you.

The greatest teachers throughout history have utilized and told us about the *Law of Attraction*. Shakespeare, Beethoven, Leonardo da Vinci, Socrates, Plato, Ralph Waldo Emerson, Sir Francis Bacon and so many others have expressed the *Law of Attraction* in their works. Religions from Buddhism to Christianity, and ancient civilizations like the Babylonians and Egyptians spread the message in their parables and stories.

Think of yourself as a vibrational magnet. The thoughts you have and more importantly, the feeling behind the thoughts you have, invoke the most powerful law in the universe, and that is the *Law of Attraction*. What you most think and feel about is what you attract.

You Attract What You Think and Feel

Imagine relaxing in front of your television and you want to watch a certain station. This TV station you want to watch is at a specific frequency so you need to dial-in to that frequency to receive the channel. If the channel you want is at 121 and you set the dial to 13, you won't get the station you want and may just get static. You have to set the TV on channel 121 to get the station you want. And, if you want to watch something different you need to change the vibrational frequency to another channel.

A *thought* is a frequency too. A thought is magnetic. A thought is a vibration you send. The *Law of Attraction* is checking the vibrational frequency of a thought, matching it, and sending it back as the television of our life. If you want to change the life you're receiving, you need to change the channel of the vibrational frequency of your ***thoughts***.

Quantum physics tell us the entire universe came from thought. What we know as reality is a creation of thought. Our thoughts are attracting all the time. It doesn't just work if you know about it. It has always been working in your life and every other person's life since the beginning of time.

When you become aware of the ***Law of Attraction***, then you can become aware of how powerful you really are. You can become deliberate in your attracting by being deliberate in your thought. You have the power to intentionally think and create your entire life with your mind!

How do we stop sending negative vibrations and attracting what we don't want? We need to hear how to change things... how to change our frequency. We need to learn how to become more deliberate in our thought. We need to learn how to become ***Deliberate Attractors***!

Getting It

Let's recap what we've just learned.

- The ***Law of Attraction*** is a Universal Law.

- The definition of the ***Law of Attraction*** is: You attract to your life whatever you give your attention, energy and focus to... whether good or bad.

- At every moment including right now, everybody has a mood or feeling. We learned that your mood or feeling actually causes you to send off a vibration.

- When we are talking about vibrations, we are also talking about frequencies and magnetic energy.

- You learned that the *Law of Attraction* is all about vibrational energy. There are two kinds of vibrations.

- The two kinds of vibrational energy are negative and positive.

- You are sending out a vibration all the time.

- At any given moment, you can tell which of the two vibrations you're sending by how you feel.

- So, that means right now you're all sending a vibration, either negative or positive. And, as you are sending this vibration, whether deliberate or not, the *Law of Attraction* is doing two things. The first thing it's doing is checking and when the *Law of Attraction* finds the vibration you're sending, it matches it.

- It matches it by giving you more of the same.

Chapter Two

Changing Your Vibration

"Oh, my God," you're thinking, "I send out negative vibes all the time without even realizing it!"

Most people are on auto-pilot and are unaware they have the power to control the thoughts in their heads. I'm going to help you change that.

Thoughts are **words** and certain words you **use** and **think** cause you to send out a negative vibration.

That's really good news, because I'm going to tell you what the words are. However, there's bad news too. The bad news is most people use these words over 150 times before noon. As I said, most people are on auto-pilot.

Words to Avoid

An easy way to stop sending out negative vibrations is to avoid certain words like **don't**, **not** and **no** and any other words of negation.

Remember, the *Law of Attraction* states whatever you give your attention, energy, and focus to will get you more of it... whether good or bad, positive or negative.

Whenever you use the words, *don't, not* and *no*, you just gave attention to what you don't want to give attention to!

Let me give you some examples.

- I *don't* want you to think of the Statue of Liberty.

- *Don't* think of the American flag.

Well, I know you thought about the Statue of Liberty and the American flag!

- *Don't* think of an apple.

- *Don't* think of the president.

Do you notice when I told you what not to do, you gave your attention, energy and focus to it?

Use your computer and go to a search engine and type in the words, *no macaroni*. What do you get pages and pages of? Sure enough, the word macaroni comes up time after time.

Every time you use the words, ***don't, not*** and ***no***, you just brought attention to what you don't want!

When you say, "I don't want to catch the flu," the universe hears, ***"I want the flu and I want to catch more things."***

"I don't want to argue," means to the universe, ***"I want more arguing."***

"I don't want a bad haircut" means, ***"I want bad haircuts."***

"I can't handle all this work" means, ***"I want more work than I can handle."***

"I don't want that person to be rude to me" means ***"I want that person and other people to be rude to me."***

The universe is very obedient. It doesn't hear any words of negation. When you focus on the things that you ***don't*** want, "I ***don't*** want to be late, please ***don't*** let me be late!" the ***Law of Attraction*** doesn't hear that you don't want it. It manifests the things that you're focused on. The universe is not biased to ***wants*** and ***don't wants***. It's job is to check and match the vibration you're offering, to check and match the things you're giving your attention to, no matter what that happens to be.

When you say 'no Statue of Liberty' or 'no American Flag' that's not going to screw up your life. But when you're talking about your goals, your dreams, your business, and your relationships, then the words you use really matter.

I hear business people say, "Don't hesitate to contact me." They just gave attention to hesitation.

"Don't forget." We just gave attention to forgetting.

"Don't be disappointed." We're really giving attention to disappointment.

When you mothers say, "Don't play ball in the house," you gave your attention to playing ball in the house.

"Don't get your clothes dirty." "Don't spill your milk." "Don't beat up your brother." "Don't do drugs." "Don't have sex." "Don't drink and drive." Have I made my point?

When we use the word *don't*, the *Law of Attraction* will just bring you more of it. So, I'm going to teach you how to stop saying *don't*, *not* and *no*.

Reframing Your Words

Here's the magic sentence to change your vibration from negative (don't wants) to positive:

So, what do I want?

Remember earlier I said, "Don't forget?" What do I want? *I want you to remember*.

"Don't play ball in the house". What do I want? *I want you to play outside*.

"I don't want this to hurt." What do I want? *I want this to feel good*.

"Don't park here." We should say, *park over there*.

'No Exit' could say, *Entrance Only*.

Any sentence in the whole wide world that has the words *don't*, *not* and *no* in it can be reframed and re-languaged with this simple sentence… *"So, what do I want?"*

When I go from what I *don't* want to what I *do* want, the words change and, when the words change… the vibration changes.

So, remember when I said, "I *don't* what to be late?" What *do* I want? *I want to be early*.

"I don't want to be disappointed." What do I want? *I want to feel pleased*.

"I don't you to be angry." What do you want? *I want you to be calm*.

You can only have one vibration at a time. When you hear yourself use the words, ***don't***, ***not*** and ***no***, in that very moment ask yourself, ***"So, what do I want?"***

How can you remember? What strategy can you use? Some people put the words on a 3x5 card, or make it their new screen saver. Or, their new password is, "So what do I want?" Or, they get a vanity license plate for their car that says, "So what do I want?"

These are all great strategies, but what if you could program your subconscious mind to bring you the change every time you said what you didn't want? Wouldn't that be great if you had a little reminder from your inner voice?

Light Switch Reset

To become more aware of the words you use imagine a light switch on the top of your head. When you're saying ***don't***, ***not*** and ***no***, your light switch is off. So tap your head to turn on the light and say, "Here's what I want!"

> ***If you can imagine it, you can achieve it. If you can dream it, you become it.***

Getting It

Here's what we learned in this chapter:

- When you go from what you ***don't*** want to what you ***do*** want, the vibration changes.

- When you change the vibration, the new vibration you're sending has changed from negative to positive.

- The ***Law of Attraction*** does not remember what yesterday's vibration was because the ***Law of Attraction*** is only checking right now.

- Everyone has an area in their lives that they would like to change from what they ***don't*** want to what they ***do*** want. You're learning how to do that by creating a light switch in your subconscious mind to change your vibrations. You're learning how to turn on the light of your positive vibrations.

- You've learned a simple sentence to reset your vibrations. And, that magic sentence is, ***"So, what do I want?"***

- When you ask yourself, "What do I want?" and you hold that focus, you are in that very moment vibrating what you desire using the most powerful force in the universe.

- The *Law of Attraction* doesn't recognize the words *don't*, *not* and *no*, or any other words of negation. Could *not* (couldn't), would *not* (wouldn't), should *not* (shouldn't), is *not* (isn't), can *not* (can't), *try* and *maybe* are words to avoid as well. People living in the south must be aware of the word, *ain't*. **The Law of Attraction** is matching what you are thinking about... always!

- You will receive significant results just by changing the words you're using, because the words you're using cause you to send a vibration. There's a reason some people call this process, *Deliberate Attraction*. You have to be *deliberate*, and deliberate in the vibrations that you send.

Do or do not, there is no try.

Chapter Three

Beginning the Manifestation Process

At every moment, including right now and right now, everybody has a mood or a feeling, and that mood or feeling is causing you to send out a vibration, even if you're not doing it on purpose.

That means that right now, we're all sending out a vibration, and in the vibrational world there are only two kinds of vibrations; negative and positive. The powerful force of the *Law of Attraction* in the universe is responding to the vibration that you're sending, by matching it and giving you more of the same vibration.

It's important to understand the *Law of Attraction* is very obedient. In other words, it will keep matching vibrations whether negative or positive. It doesn't make judgments about what's right or wrong, and it doesn't keep you out of trouble! As you're giving your attention, energy, and focus to something that you *don't* want, the universe is obediently unfolding and orchestrating people, events and things to give you more of what you *don't* want! Conversely, when you give energy and attention to what you *do* want you will obediently receive the same.

We learned that one of the main reasons people keep attracting what they don't want is because of what they say. The words *don't, not, no* and any others of negation cause an attraction of the very things we are pushing against. The words we use and the thoughts that we think cause us to send a vibration, and every time we use any words that negate, at that very moment, we give attention, energy, and focus to that which we said we didn't want.

But, now you have a correction tool. You have a tool to help reset your vibration. If you don't like the results you are getting, and you've learned the results that you get are a result of the vibrations that you send, and the vibrations that you send are a result of the thoughts that you think; then change your thoughts, which will change the vibration and in turn, change the results. That's called resetting your vibration and turning on your subconscious light switch.

There's an easy and quick way to reset your vibration. As soon as you hear yourself using the words, don't, not and no, say, "So, what do I want?" or "Here's what I want!"

When you go from what you don't want to what you do want, the words change, and when the words change the vibration changes and you can only have one vibration at a time.

We call this deliberate attraction. You can call it deliberate creation, or deliberate manifestation, creative manifestation, or goal setting… whatever that may be.

A lot of traditional goal setting or manifestation techniques teach you to build a list of what you want and then *put it out* to the universe. Well, how do you put it out there? Where do I put it? What does that mean, put it out there?

There are 3 main steps to deliberately attract what you want and use the *Law of Attraction* to your advantage.

Step #1: Identify Desire (What Do I Want?)

Traditional goal setting involves building a list of what we desire, but that's not always easy. Most people have trouble determining what they want, but they're very good at knowing what they *don't* want. Actually, knowing what you don't want *is* important. In fact, it's essential for helping you determine what it is you *do* want.

For example when you look at the television schedule and note what you don't want to watch, you then decide on what you do want to watch. Knowing and making that *choice* about what doesn't feel good or knowing what you don't want is essential. It gives you clarity about what you *do* want. But, there's a key length of time to observe it and it's different for everyone. When looking at a restaurant menu, most people will observe what they don't like for a minute or two. On the other hand, when it comes to relationships for example, some people may observe what they don't want for many years.

The key length of time to observe what you don't want is *briefly*.

You know you ***don't*** want it if it doesn't *feel* good.

The Story of Dave

I have a friend, Dave, who's in business, and every time I talk to him he's always complaining about his business. "Business is slow. Nobody is buying stuff. People don't keep appointments." And of course we know why, don't we? He's talking about what he doesn't want and giving his full attention, energy and focus to it!

The Law of Polarity

So, Dave and I go to lunch and I take one of those paper placemats from the table and turn it over and draw a line down the middle. Across the top of the paper I had Dave write; *My Ideal Client*.

On the top of one column I had Dave write; ***Feels Bad*** and on the other column; ***Feels Good***. You see, noticing the difference in how you *feel* is essential to getting clear about what you want. I am going to teach Dave how to use the ***Law of Polarity*** to determine what he wants.

I had Dave write down ten things that he didn't like or want about his clients. Here are some things Dave wrote down in the *Feels Bad* column concerning his clients.

"What I Want Worksheet"	
Name: Dave	
My Ideal Client	
FEELS BAD	**FEELS GOOD**
Looks but doesn't buy	
Doesn't return phone calls	
Does not commit	
Does not pay on time	
Changes their mind	
Cancels appointments	
Not intelligent	
Doesn't do the work	
Doesn't show up	
Does not buy again	
>>>>> **This is what I want** >>>>>	

It's best to list 50-100 things on this list and it may take an hour or two to complete. This worksheet can be updated frequently as you'll probably think of more things you don't want. This was just a short list to get Dave started. The more things you list about what you don't want will give you a better idea of what you do want. Here's how it works!

I asked Dave the magic question, "So, what do you want?" Then, I had Dave write under the *Feels Good* column what he did want and had him cross out each item from the *Feels Bad* column as he invoked the *Law of Polarity* and got clear about what he wanted. The *Law of Polarity* helps Dave become clear of the kind of client he wants and this is how his worksheet looked.

"What I Want Worksheet"	
Name: Dave	
My Ideal Client	
FEELS BAD	**FEELS GOOD**
Looks but doesn't buy	Clients that buy
Doesn't return phone calls	They call back
Does not commit	Clients that commit
Does not pay on time	Customers that pay on time
Changes their mind	Decisive clients
Cancels appointments	They keep appointments
Not intelligent	Understand and process well
Doesn't do the work	Clients that do the work
Doesn't show up	Customers that show up
Does not buy again	Repeat buyers
>>>>> This is what I want >>>>>	

Is this what Dave wants? Is this what Dave is now vibrating? Dave is getting clarity about what he desires and can now give his attention, energy, and focus to what he wants instead of what he doesn't. This exercise helps determine what you want by *briefly* observing what you don't want.

I know I told you not to focus on negativity, but *briefly* focusing on what you *don't* want will help you determine what you *do* want, and by giving your attention, energy and focus to what you *do* want, the vibrations you send change, and the *Law of Attraction* can match your desire.

Would that *What I Want* worksheet of Dave's make a good client? Yes, and by updating his list periodically with more *don't wants* and *do wants*, Dave can attract an even better client!

You need at least 50-100 things on your worksheet. The more things you can reframe to the positive side, the more power and passion your intentions, wants, and desires will be and the clearer you will be in deliberately offering what you want.

The *What I Want* worksheet will work for any area in your life; relationships, health, financial, etc. You can fine-tune it to any category. For example in the relationships category, you can use the worksheet for, My Ideal Mate, Partner, Parent, Child, Friend, Co-Worker, Employee, etc. Do you see where I'm going with this?

The Story of Angie

My friend Angie wanted an ideal relationship. She had a good idea of what she didn't want from looking at her past relationships and needed to work with the *Law of Polarity* using a *What I Want* worksheet to attract what she wanted in an ideal mate. Here are some things Angie put on the negative and positive sides of her list.

"What I Want Worksheet"	
Name: Angie	
My Ideal Relationship	
FEELS BAD	FEELS GOOD
Not affectionate	Affectionate, sensitive
Doesn't call	Keeps in contact
Does not commit	Wants a committed relationship
Does not pay for dinner	Pays for dinner and dates
Changes their mind	Decisive, can make up mind
Works too much	Balances work and play
Won't open door	Opens door, gallant
Doesn't listen	Great listening skills
Doesn't show up	Dependable
Does not like to travel	Likes travel and adventure
>>>>> This is what I want >>>>>	

Using an expanded worksheet with 50-100 items will help Angie get clear about what she wants and will help her stop negatively focusing on what she doesn't want.

A realtor could use this technique when selling a house. Most home-buyers don't know what they want, but they sure know what they don't want, especially first time buyers. You could have them write down what they don't want on the negative side, reframe the words on the positive side and presto, the buyers now have a clear idea about what they want!

Could a travel agent use the *What I Want* worksheet to determine her client's perfect vacation? Yes, the client could list everything they didn't like about their previous vacations and better determine what they want this time; too cold / sunny moderate climate; rude people / warm inviting people; etc.

You already use this technique when you go to a restaurant and look at the menu. "This is fried, I don't want fish, this has too many carbs, too much fat in this… yes; I think I'll have a salad!" Through a brief observation of contrast, you can arrive at clarity about what you want. This technique will work in any area of business and any area of your life. Knowing what you *don't* want is essential to knowing what you *do* what.

Change your thoughts and change your world.

The Story of Bill

A client of mine, Bill, was having a difficult time with his finances. He was always complaining about not having enough money. He was stressed and felt so bad, he wasn't able to sleep. Does Bill sound like someone you know? Remember, in Bill's worksheet below I've listed 10 items as an example. He needs to list 50-100 items to get really clear about what he wants.

"What I Want Worksheet"	
Name: Bill	
My Ideal Financial	
FEELS BAD	**FEELS GOOD**
Always have bills	Bills are paid quickly
Can't make enough money	More than enough money
Does not win anything	Wins prizes & receives gifts
Makes the same pay weekly	Money from various sources
Struggles with mortgage	House payment is made easily
Stressed-out about money	Money is a good friend
Money does not come easy	Money comes easily to me
Can't afford things	Always have enough money
Not enough money	An abundance of money
No money to travel	Plenty of money to enjoy life
>>>>> **This is what I want** >>>>>	

Using the *What I Want* worksheet and the *Law of Polarity* will help you with Step #1 of the *Deliberate Manifestation* process which simply is; *What Do I Want?*

Getting It

In this chapter we learned how to identify desire.

- Step #1 of the *Deliberate Manifestation* process is; *Identify Desire*

- Most people don't know what they want. They are focused on what they don't want.

- We used the *Law of Polarity* and the *What I Want* worksheet to help us identify what we want.

- The more items you list on the *What I Want* worksheet, the clearer you will be about your desire. I suggest a minimum of 50-100.

- Anyone could use this technique in any area of life from identifying an ideal romantic relationship to identifying an ideal vacation.

Before we move on to Step #2 of the *Deliberate Manifestation* process, let's learn more about vibrations.

There is only one corner of the universe you can be certain of improving and that's your own self.

Chapter Four

The Vibrational Aura

As you are becoming clear about your desire by deliberately thinking about what you don't want and writing what you do want on your *What I Want* worksheet, you're giving it positive vibrations which set the energy in motion. You're actually including the vibration in something called the *Vibrational Aura*.

Imagine an energy field surrounding you and inside this field of energy are all the vibrations you send out. The *Law of Attraction* is checking and matching the vibrations you hold in your *Vibrational Aura*.

Your goals and desires are outside of this energy field because you haven't received them yet. The next step to attracting the life you want is *including* the desire you've identified with Step #1 of the *Deliberate Manifestation* process, inside your *Vibrational Aura*. We do this by giving our desire attention, energy and focus.

If you build your worksheet, become clear about what you want, and then put it away in a drawer, the *Law of*

Attraction won't match it because you're not giving any attention to what you desire. It only responds to what you're focused on and holding in your *Vibrational Aura*.

In a moment you'll learn how to use *words* to create a *Statement of Desire*. By giving attention, energy and focus to our *Statement of Desire*, we include the vibration in our *Vibrational Aura* and the *Law of Attraction* responds to it.

You're including it in your *Vibrational Aura* when you're talking about your desire, when you're visualizing your desire, when you're praying about your desire, and many other positive ways. You're also including it in your *Vibrational Aura* when you're worrying about it, and complaining about not having it!

Step #2: Give Desire Attention

To most people, Step #2 of *Deliberate Manifestation* is somewhat new.

How many times have you heard motivational speakers, goal-setting teachers, and life-coaches say to make your list of what you want in your life and send it out to the universe and wait until it comes to you? So, you work on your list of what you want and that's great because you're giving it a lot of attention and focus, but, then you put it in your drawer and forget about it.

Remember, the *Law of Attraction* states, I attract to my life whatever I give my energy, attention, and focus to. How can you give any energy to your desires if they're sitting in the back of a drawer? You need to give it attention! Now you can understand another reason you're not getting what you want. Step #2 of the *Deliberate Manifestation* process is, *Give Desire Attention*, and by giving your wants and desires attention you raise your vibration and include it in your *Vibrational Aura*.

Now, there's lots of ways to do this. You can visualize, celebrate it, make a screen saver to run on your computer, etc. These are good to help focus your thoughts, but thoughts are made up of words and the best way to give your desire attention, energy and focus is to use *words*.

Creating a Statement of Desire

"Thank you! I'm in the process of attracting all that I need to do, know, and have to attract my ideal... (client, body, financial situation, etc.)

There are two important words in the above statement; *process* and *ideal*.

When does the *process* start? Right *now*! You're setting the energy in motion right now.

A good way to include our desires in our *Vibrational Auras* and give what we want attention, energy and focus, is to create a 3-Part *Statement of Desire* which starts with a *believable* opening statement.

Part #1 Create an Opening Statement

Just by saying, "Thank you! I'm in the *process* of attracting all that I need to do, know, and have to attract my *ideal* (blank)" sets the energy in motion. By stating your wants and desires like this, you can *believe* what you're saying.

Here's why affirmations don't work. They're not true! You can't believe what you're saying. Affirmations don't say the word *ideal*. They state something that isn't true yet. The statement doesn't *feel true* and it doesn't *feel good*. Remember, it's all about the feeling behind the words.

When you state something that isn't true for you and doesn't feel right, you are sending out a negative vibration.

- I'm a millionaire. No, that's not true. I'm not a millionaire.

- My business is successful. No, that's not true. My business is failing.

- I have perfect health. No, that's not true. My back is always hurting.

- I enjoy a wonderful relationship. No, that's not true. My boyfriend treats me badly.

If someone needs to lose 50 lbs. and stands in front of the mirror and says an affirmation, "I'm so happy and slender in my new healthy body," the little voice inside his head is saying, "No, you liar! You're a big fat pig!"

But, if they said, "Thank you! I'm in the *process* of attracting all that I need to do, know, and have to attract my *ideal* healthy body," they would be saying a positive, believable statement that wouldn't be diluted by any negative statements inside your head.

You can see how a positive affirmation can have a negative vibration attached to it. It doesn't feel true and believable.

Take our example of the person who wants to lose 50 lbs. Affirmations don't work here because of the *feeling*. Affirmation words we use don't necessarily match the vibration we're holding in our *Vibrational Aura*.

Part #2 Create Item Statements

Once you have written your opening statement, the next step is to create believable statements about the items you listed on the *Feels Good* side of your *What I Want* worksheet.

Here are some great statements to use:

- I love how it feels when…
- I love knowing that my ideal…
- I love the thought of…
- I choose…
- I'm excited about the thought of…
- I love the idea of…
- I've decided…

"What I Want Worksheet"	
Name: Dave	
My Ideal Client	
FEELS BAD	FEELS GOOD
Looks but doesn't buy	Clients that buy
Doesn't return phone calls	They call back
Does not commit	Clients that commit
Does not pay on time	Customers that pay on time
Changes their mind	Decisive clients
Cancels appointments	They keep appointments
Not intelligent	Understand and process well
Doesn't do the work	Clients that do the work
Doesn't show up	Customers that show up
Does not buy again	Repeat buyers
>>>>> This is what I want >>>>>	

Let's go back to Dave's worksheet from the last chapter and see how he can hold a raised positive vibration about his ideal client.

Dave simply states (and writes), "Thank you! I am in the process of attracting all that I need to do, know, and have to attract my ideal client. I love how it feels knowing that my clients *show up on time*. I love knowing that my clients *pay me on time*." He goes down his list and makes a positive believable statement for each item. "I love the thought of *repeat buyers*. I love the idea of communicating with clients who are *intelligent*."

As you're writing about your desire, you're giving it positive energy which sets the energy in motion. The *Law of Attraction* doesn't respond to the words you use or the thoughts you think. It responds to how you *feel* about the words and thoughts you think. If you use the words, *in the process of* and *ideal* when you say and write your desire, you can *believe* what you're stating, and if you believe it, it feels right, it feels true and good, and sends a positive vibration to the universe.

And, speaking of the words you use, a lot of teachers say, "Don't use the word *want* cause it means you're coming from a place of lack or not having it." Remember, it's about the way we *feel* about the words we use.

When I whine the words, "I want one of those," it feels bad and I'm sending out a negative vibration. But, when I say the same words with passion and excitement, "Wow! I want one of those!" I am sending positive vibrations.

It's not the words you use, its how you *feel* about the words you use. When you change the words you use to words you can believe and feel good about, you vibrate a wonderful positive energy that the *Law of Attraction* can check and respond to. Next, we need to complete our *Statement of Desire* with a closing statement.

Part #3 Create the Closing Statement

Completing your *Statement of Desire* sets the vibration in motion. A believable closing statement I like to use is:

> *"The Law of Attraction is matching my vibrational energy and doing what needs to be done to manifest my desire. I now allow myself the manifestation of my ideal (<u>blank</u>)."*

These powerful words complete your *Statement of Desire* and start the vibrational energies in motion.

Let's take a look at Angie's.

Angie's Statement of Desire

Using Angie's *What I Want* worksheet let's make a *Statement of Desire*.

Opening Statement

"Thank you! I'm in the process of attracting all that I need to do, know and have to attract my ideal relationship."

"What I Want Worksheet"	
Name: Angie	
My Ideal Relationship	
FEELS BAD	**FEELS GOOD**
Not affectionate	Affectionate, sensitive
Doesn't call	Keeps in contact
Does not commit	Wants a committed relationship
Does not pay for dinner	Pays for dinner and dates
Changes their mind	Decisive, can make up mind
Works too much	Balances work and play
Won't open door	Opens door, gallant
Doesn't listen	Great listening skills
Doesn't show up	Dependable
Does not like to travel	Likes travel and adventure
>>>>> **This is what I want** >>>>>	

Item Statements

"I love knowing that my ideal relationship is with a man who is affectionate and sensitive. He pays for dinner and dates and always opens the door for me."

"I'm excited at the thought of traveling with my ideal partner and having wonderful adventures. I love how it feels to know my ideal man wants a committed relationship. How he balances work and play, and how he listens to what I have to say."

"I've decided my ideal relationship is with a man who is dependable, keeps in contact with me and is decisive."

Closing Statement

"The Law of Attraction is matching my vibrational energy and doing what needs to be done to manifest my desire. I now allow myself the manifestation of my ideal relationship."

Let's do another.

Bill's Statement of Desire

Opening Statement

"Thank you! I'm in the process of attracting all that I need to do, know and have to attract my ideal financial situation."

Item Statements

"I'm so excited at the thought of having plenty of money to enjoy life. I love the thought of paying my mortgage on time and being stress-free about money. I love the feeling of abundance in my life where my bills are paid easily and money is a friend. I'm so excited at the thought of winning prizes and receiving gifts. I love the feeling of receiving income from different sources."

"What I Want Worksheet"	
Name: Bill	
My Ideal Financial Situation	
FEELS BAD	**FEELS GOOD**
Always have bills	Bills are paid quickly
Can't make enough money	More than enough money
Does not win anything	Wins prizes & receives gifts
Makes the same pay weekly	Money from various sources
Struggles with mortgage	House payment is made easily
Stressed-out about money	Money is a good friend
Money does not come easy	Money comes easily to me
Can't afford things	Always have enough money
Not enough money	An abundance of money
No money to travel	Plenty of money to enjoy life
>>>>> This is what I want >>>>>	

Closing Statement

"The Law of Attraction is matching my vibrational energy and doing what needs to be done to manifest my desire. I now allow myself the manifestation of my ideal financial situation"

These are a couple of examples to illustrate the process. You start with the *Opening Statement*, move on the *Items* from the positive side of your *What Do I Want* worksheet, and end with the *Closing Statement*.

When you make your *Statement of Desire*, read it over a few times and see how it makes you feel. If you feel some of it as untrue, go back and rewrite that section until you can say your *Statement of Desire* and it feels true and good. The purpose of your *Statement of Desire* is to raise your vibration and include it in your *Vibrational Aura.*

Getting It

Let's recap what you've learned.

- What you think about and how you feel create vibrations that you hold in an energy field that surrounds you called the *Vibrational Aura*.

- It is important that the vibrations that are held in your *Vibrational Aura* are positive and in harmony with your desires.

- Creating a *Statement of Desire* allows us to give attention, energy and focus to what we want and thereby include it in our *Vibrational Aura*.

- Your *Statement of Desire* must include believable statements. Words like *'in the process of'* and *'my ideal'* are believable and feel good.

- Use the items from the positive side of your *What I Want* worksheet when creating your *Statement of Desire*.

- The *Closing Statement* sets the energy in motion and allows the *Law of Attraction* to match the vibrations you're holding in your *Vibrational Aura*.

Nothing can make you feel inferior without your consent.

Chapter Five

Allowing

There's a reason why the *Law of Attraction* is called *Deliberate Attraction*. It means we need to do something *deliberately*.

So when I change the words, don't, not and no to what I do want, that's deliberate. When I convert from what I don't want to what I do want, that's deliberate.

Let's take another look at our 3-step formula to deliberately attract what we want.

1. **Identify Desire**
2. **Give Desire Attention**
3. **Allow It (Allowing)**

An easy way to identify our desire is using the *Law of Polarity* and the *What Do I Want* worksheet. This allows us to get clear on what we want by briefly observing what we don't want and then reframing our *don't want* list to our *do want* list.

We then learned we need to give our desire attention, energy and focus. Some ways we can do that are making a collage or vision board and writing in a journal. These are fine as long as we give our attention to them and not put them aside or in a drawer and forget about them. That's not giving focus to our wants and desires.

The easiest way to give our desires attention is by re-framing our thoughts and changing the words we use to help focus on our desire. When we find ourselves using the words, don't, not and no, we simply reframe the negating words and sentences we use to, "So, what do I want?"

We know our wants and desires are outside of our vibration or *Vibrational Aura* because we don't have them yet. We need to learn how to bring what we want into our *Vibrational Aura* and into our reality.

"Well, I did that! I got all excited and made a collage, and prayed, and I made a cool screen saver and it hasn't shown up!" Here's the reason many people have trouble attracting their wants and desires.

Allowing is the most difficult part of the 3-step formula. Allowing is the least understood part and… it's the most important part!

> *The speed at which the Law of Attraction will manifest desire is in direct proportion to how much you are allowing.*

Do you need to read your ***Statement of Desire*** over and over again? The answer would be yes if it was only a 2-step formula.

1. **Identify Desire**
2. **Give Desire Attention**

Step 3, ***Allowing***, is our focus because allowing means we have no doubt our desires will manifest.

- Doubt equals a negative vibration.

- Desire equals a positive vibration.

- Doubt cancels desire.

What causes doubt? Blockages, limiting beliefs, fears, negativity and the absence of proof.

Imagine we had a vibrational meter and the reading for the needle could go from +1 to +10 on the positive side, and -1 to -10 on the negative side.

Let's say you've identified your ideal relationship and you know how good it feels building your ***What Do I Want*** list and you're all pumped up about it.

You're pretending and noticing and so excited about attracting that ideal relationship. On the positive side of our vibrational meter's scale of +1 to +10, your vibration would read +10.

You can tell that your vibrations are +10 by how you *feel*. You're feeling great!

Then a couple of hours later you get this little voice in your head saying, "Who do you think you are? You want to get a boyfriend or girlfriend like that?"

That little voice inside your head is the voice of *doubt*.

On the negative side of the vibrational scale from -1 to -10, that little voice of strong doubt is at -10.

On the positive side you have a +10 for desire and on the negative side you have -10 for doubt.

You do the math. Our vibration is *zero*!

Strong desire plus strong doubt equals *no* manifestation.

Strong desire and some doubt equals *slow* or *partial* manifestation. Some of the doubt has diluted some of the desire so only partial desire can come to you.

You will get *instant* manifestation with strong desire and no doubt.

Have you ever been going through your pockets or a drawer and come upon an old friend's business card and you think, "Joe, Joe, Joe, I wonder what's up with Joe?" Then you put Joe's business card on the table and go about your day.

This simple act has included Joe in your *Vibrational Aura*.

Later on you see the business card on the table and think, Joe, Joe, Joe again. You've offered the vibration of Joe again.

The speed at which the *Law of Attraction* will manifest what you give your attention, energy and focus to is always determined by how much negativity or doubt you have in receiving it (allowing it).

Since you thought about Joe and tossed his business card on the table and went about your day, you're not having any negativity or doubt concerning him.

And then before you know it, the telephone rings and Joe is on the line and you're saying, "Wow, is this ever a coincidence! I was thinking about you earlier today!"

Coincidence is evidence of the *Law of Attraction* checking and matching the vibrations you're holding in your *Vibrational Aura*. Words and statements like *serendipity, out of the blue, how weird,* are all evidence of the *Law of Attraction* checking and matching your vibrations.

People say there's no such thing as *coincidence*. If there was no such thing as coincidence, why would we need a name to call it something? If there was no dog, you wouldn't need the word *dog* to describe what wasn't there.

Negative vibrations like resistance, doubt, and fear set up a vibrational block and resistance to attracting what you want. These negative vibrations will slow or even stop manifesting your desires.

In addition, having strong desire alone won't make our desires manifest any faster. What does? *Removing* doubt will help you manifest your desires quickly.

So you ask, "Do I need to remove all the doubt to manifest?" No, the quick answer is; you need to lessen them.

Getting Rid of Doubt

How do we lessen or get rid of doubt? It's pretty clear that having strong desire doesn't make it manifest any faster and what we really need to do is get rid of doubt.

So, it's not *desire* that we need now. We've done that by getting clear of what we want with Step #1. We need to lessen or get rid of doubt.

So, that really raises the next question. How do I get rid of doubt? This may be the most important thing you learn in the *Deliberate Attraction* process.

How do you get rid of doubt? How do you **allow** your desires to manifest? The best way to remove doubt is to find *proof*. Having proof removes doubt.

Most of you know about scientists. Let's say they're gathered around this Petri dish watching an experiment. Scientists are typically very skeptical. A junior scientist is trying to get the others to buy into what he wants to show them and they say, "There's no way, we do not believe it." They're skeptical because they don't have any *proof*.

And then, the junior scientist does something and the cells split in front of them and the senior scientists all got to witness it. As soon as they saw evidence (proof), their doubt disappeared. They couldn't be convinced of anything other than what they just saw. My point is scientists are skeptical until they find proof and typically, most people are skeptical until proof removes their doubt.

If I said I could hold my breath under water for 10 minutes you'd say, "I doubt it." But, what if I did it, what would you say then? Probably something like, "You're good, Mr. Fish!"

Do you see how proof removes doubt?

Let's go back to our friend, Angie. She goes out on a date wanting to find her ideal boyfriend. There are 20 things from her **What Do I Want** list that she's looking for in her ideal man and this guy only matched 3 things.

When Angie got home from her date I asked her how it went. She started to complain, "It was horrible! He was this and this and this!" So of course, all the time she was complaining about what she didn't like about her date she's including what she didn't want in her *Vibrational Aura* and offering it to the *Law of Attraction*.

The following simple, yet dynamic tools are a terrific way to keep positive vibrations in your *Vibrational Aura* and help to lessen doubt. Remember, removing doubt by establishing proof allows the universe to manifest your desires. It is essential to believe without a doubt you will get your wish!

Tool #1: Celebrate

Celebrate in the moment the closeness of the match. Be thankful. What matched Angie's desires? She got 3 things out of 20. He was kind and generous. He paid for dinner. Angie needs to keep focusing on the things she *liked* about the date instead of what she didn't!

Using this tool, Angie is maintaining and offering the positive energy of what she liked and received from the *Law of Attraction*, and celebrating in the moment. She is slowly removing doubt that her desire will manifest.

Focus on, celebrate and be thankful for the positive things that are matching your desire, no matter how few. The *Law of Attraction* has no choice but to match what you are celebrating and bring you more.

Tool #2: Record Evidence

Every day start to notice the things about your desire that you're starting to manifest. Maybe Angie noticed some guy flirting with her at the mailbox or someone held the door open for her at the grocery store. Maybe she ran into an old boyfriend or saw some people kissing in the park.

When Angie celebrates in the moment, she's giving her desire attention, energy and focus. Then every night she can record these things in her journal.

When you record the things you've noticed that were a close match to your desire in your journal, you're duplicating all you saw today and keeping it in your vibration. The *Law of Attraction* doesn't know if you're remembering, pretending, or playing. It doesn't matter though; the *Law of Attraction* is picking up on the vibration you're sending.

By recording evidence in your journal, you're spending 10 minutes in the vibration of the way you want it to be, which is better than spending no time at all.

Most people don't spend any time focusing on how they want it to be. All of their focus is on how they don't want it to be! When you're noticing and celebrating the closeness of your matches and recording them in your journal, you're including the vibration in your *Vibrational Aura* and you are doing it *deliberately*. This tool helps you with Step #3, *Allowing* and makes you a *Deliberate Attractor*.

When Angie goes on another date, when she gets home she needs to check off her list and record the matches again. In other words, she needs to deliberately keep noticing and including the evidence in her vibrations.

You'll know when you find enough matches because you'll feel really good. Right! You can tell by how you *feel*.

The universe has given us a wonderful tool to help us determine if our thoughts and vibrations are in alignment with our desires. It's called our *Emotions*.

When you're feeling good, your emotions are letting you know you're connected and in alignment with your wants and desires. When you're feeling bad the opposite is true, and you need to change your thoughts until you can feel good and stay positive in your vibration!

The important thing to know is that you can't hold a bad feeling and a good thought at the same time. If you are feeling bad, it's because you are thinking thoughts that are making you *feel* bad. If you are feeling good, it is because you are thinking good thoughts that are in alignment with what you want. When you're celebrating those desires you're starting to attract, you're feeling good and including that feeling in your *Vibrational Aura*.

Tool 3: What I Like About (blank)

In Angie's case, another tool she could use to help remove doubt is to notice what she likes about other men in her life, like her father, brother, male friends, etc. and include these additional qualities in her vibrations.

"Here's what I like about my father. He's funny and likes to cook Sunday breakfast."

The things she likes about her father that weren't on her ideal relationship *What I Want* worksheet can be added and included in her *Vibrational Aura*.

She can build a list about what she likes about her mailman, and what she likes about the guy in the coffee shop, or her favorite teacher from college. This tool helps with gathering characteristics Angie likes about different men in her life and helps to bring even more clarity to what she wants.

When you include the vibration, you'll get what you've included. You don't get what you want, you get what you include… and you get it by how you *feel* about it.

Allowing is believing, and believing involves acting, speaking, and thinking as though you have already received what you have asked for. When you're offering the vibration of having received your desire, the *Law of Attraction* unfolds and brings you the people, events, opportunities and inspired inspiration for you to manifest what you want.

Allowing involves feeling the way you will feel once you have received your desire.

Getting It

In this chapter we learned about the 3rd Step in the *Deliberate Manifestation* process; *Allowing*.

- Allowing is the most difficult, most important, and most misunderstood part of the 3-Step *Deliberate Manifestation* process.

- Allowing is the process of removing doubt which blocks the *Law of Attraction* from matching your desire.

- We've learned that doubt equals a negative vibration, causes resistance and cancels out our positive desires.

- Having proof lessens and removes doubt.

- There are three tools to help us remove doubt: *Celebrating*, *Recording Evidence* and the *What I Like About (blank)* tool.

We'll be covering more tools and techniques for removing doubts, releasing negativity and letting go of limiting beliefs in later chapters.

Chapter Six

Identifying Limiting Beliefs

You're working hard on creating the life you want. You have your *Statement of Desire* fine-tuned to include your ideals when it comes to all areas of your life, be it relationships, health, work, career and money.

You're noticing some success, lots of success, and definitely less of what you don't want because you're more deliberate in your thoughts and the vibrations you're sending out to the universe. However, some things aren't manifesting at all.

"What am I doing wrong?" you ask.

Right and wrong, are words we use to describe what we *believe* about something. You're really not *doing* something wrong. You're doing everything right but feeling something is wrong; something that you're not even aware of. Most likely, it's a limited belief you have.

Think back to when you were growing up. Who would you say had the most influence on you? Mom? Dad? Was it you're grandparents, a teacher from school or the preacher from church? Maybe your siblings had a big influence on you. Friends I had growing up had a big influence on me.

Most people would say Mom is the number one influence and Dad is most likely second. But, whoever this major influence in your life was (maybe still is) would be a good starting place to figure out why some things are either not manifesting for you or coming very slowly.

First of all we're not going to blame your Mom and I'm going to use the word "Mom" to include whoever your major influence was, because Mom is our source of nurturing, teaching, and guidance. She's the person we look up to and unfortunately, our first source of limiting beliefs.

Now Mom told you a lot of things about life and how to live it. Since (s)he was your authority figure, you believed just about everything (s)he told you. But, let's not forget "Mom" only told you things that (s)he was told by her/his "Mom."

Maybe you were told things like, "Money is evil and rich people are cheap and dishonest." Remember hearing things like, "You have to work hard to have anything, life is difficult and you must be prepared for disappointment because no one in our family ever amounted to anything."

Does this sound familiar? "Don't follow your pie-in-the-sky dreams, get a real job because life is a struggle and you need to have a good job and security."

All these little seeds have been planted in your subconscious mind and have matured into full-grown compulsive limiting beliefs.

- I can't.
- Because.
- That's silly.
- I've tried before.

Do you use these words? How do you feel when you say them?

You know, Henry Ford said, "Whether you think you can or you think you can't, either way you are right." Limiting beliefs are similar to computer viruses running in our subconscious minds ready and waiting to sabotage the manifesting of our desires and wishes.

You always get what you wish for. When you state your wish; "Thank you! I'm in the process of attaining my ideal weight" (positive), and a little voice inside you is saying, "I can't lose weight because everyone in my family has trouble losing weight and keeping it off" (negative), you've just sent off conflicting vibrations and the *Law of Attraction* isn't going to manifest your desires.

> *Don't let the past dictate who you are, let it dictate who you will become.*

Here are some more examples of limiting beliefs:

- "I'd like to write a book, but I can't because I don't have a degree in English Literature."

- "I want a loving relationship, but I can't because I'm too shy and have trouble talking to the opposite sex."

- "I want to be wealthy, but I have to be dishonest and take advantage of people to become so."

Limiting beliefs send out negative vibrations. Limiting beliefs are another reason the "Allowing" step of the 3-Step *Deliberate Manifestation* process is difficult for most people. Limiting beliefs imply doubt, and doubt is removed by establishing proof. When you have proof, your beliefs change, and when you change your beliefs, your vibrations change from negative to positive. Now, everything fueling your *Statement of Desire* is in vibrational harmony and the *Law of Attraction* can do its job and bring what you want.

One tool we can use to help change limiting beliefs and lessen or remove doubt are *Allowing Statements* which are discussed in the next chapter. Using this tool will help change your beliefs and more importantly, how you feel about your beliefs. You will feel less resistance, more relaxed, relieved, and because you will be removing doubt, you can truly *believe* you will attract what you desire.

As more and more of your desires are manifesting, make a journal and each day write all the people, events and things that you are attracting to your life and refer to your journal often as further proof of your deliberate manifesting. As you have learned, having proof removes doubt. Your journal is a record of evidence.

It is essential to change your limiting negative beliefs to positive thoughts. Offering these new positive thoughts over and over will create a new belief system instead of the belief system 'Mom' gave you.

"Mom, I forgive you. I know you love me and only taught me the beliefs your Mom told you. But, I'm a little stressed about the limiting beliefs we are programmed with by television, religion, books, magazines, celebrities, friends, governments, the medical profession..."

Getting It

Here's what we learned about *Limiting Beliefs*.

- Limited beliefs are introduced by our most influential person when growing up, usually Mom or Dad.

- Limited beliefs can also be learned from our friends and family today as well as TV, newspapers and the media.

- One cause of slow, limited or no manifestation is limited beliefs.

- Similar to computer viruses running in our subconscious, limited beliefs sabotage our desires.

- Limited beliefs send out negative vibrations and imply doubt.

Wisdom is divided into two parts: 1. Having a great deal to say, and 2. not saying it.

Chapter Seven

Allowing Statements

Changing our limiting beliefs and removing doubt helps with the *Allowing* step of the 3-Step formula for *Deliberate Manifestation*; Step #1 *Identify Desire*, Step #2 *Give Desire Attention*, Step #3 *Allowing*

A tool you can use to change or eliminate limiting beliefs is called the statement of allowing or *Allowing Statements*. There are 4 steps to creating an *Allowing Statement*.

1. **Start by asking yourself if anyone else on the planet is doing what you want or has what you want.**

2. **Put a number on how many people already have or are doing what you desire; 100, 1,000, 10,000, a million.**

3. **Always write your Allowing Statement using the 3rd person. It is important for you to stay on the sideline observing.**

4. Make sure the Allowing Statement you write is plausible.

Limiting Belief Example #1

"I want to have a warm, loving relationship, but I can't because I'm too shy and can't talk to the opposite sex."

Question: Is anyone on Earth able to talk easily to the opposite sex?

Answer: Yes.

Question: Of the millions and millions of people on the planet, how many can easily talk to the opposite sex?

Allowing Statement

Millions of people on the planet can easily talk with the opposite sex. There are thousands of people who have easily talked with people of the opposite sex since time began. Hundreds of people are enjoying stimulating conversation with the opposite sex at this very moment.

Limiting Belief Example #2

"I want to write a book, but I can't because I'm too old."

Question: Is there anyone on this planet my age that is writing books?

Answer: Yes

Question: How many people are writing books at my age?

Allowing Statement

Right now, there are thousands of people in their 50's who write books. There are countless numbers of successful people in their 50's who write books every year. Hundreds of books are being written by people in their 50's right now.

Remember Angie and Bill we talked about earlier? Let's take a look at the *Allowing Statements* they created.

Angie is frustrated when it comes to finding her ideal relationship because she keeps attracting men who are either unavailable, insensitive, or won't commit. She is using the *Deliberate Manifestation* process to help attract her ideal mate but is finding some resistance. Angie is clear on her *Statement of Desire* (Step #1) and knows what kind of mate she wants and the qualities she desires in a man. She is giving her desire energy, attention and focus (Step #2) by using her vision board, writing in her journal and celebrating everything she notices manifesting about her desire.

There may be some issues and resistance with Step #3, *Allowing*, because Angie's desire hasn't manifested yet. She needs to create an *Allowing Statement* to help remove doubt and limiting beliefs caught in her *Vibrational Aura*.

Angie's Allowing Statement

Hundreds of people met their ideal partner last month. Thousands of people on the planet are enjoying being with a person today who will become their lifelong mate. Hundreds of thousands of couples are together today lovingly enjoying each others company. Every day more and more people are attracting their ideal partner. Millions of people are in committed, loving relationships and spending quality time together.

When Angie reads her *Allowing Statement*, she begins to remove doubt and limiting beliefs and the *Law of Attraction* can bring Angie her desire.

Remember Bill? He's using the *Law of Attraction* to ease his financial burden. He's always complaining and stressed about money and meeting his bills. He feels he's working too hard just to get by.

Bill is clear about what he desires (Step #1) and he is giving his attention, energy and focus (Step #2) to what he wants. However, he needs to lessen doubt and the limited beliefs he's learned about money in order to attract and allow his ideal financial situation (Step #3) to manifest.

Bill's Allowing Statement

Millions of people are receiving money every day. Currency exchanges hands thousands and thousands of times daily. Bank to bank, business to business, and person to person, money is constantly moving. Somebody received a check just this minute. Money is inherited, found, and given away every day. Thousands of people earn money from jobs they enjoy and many are operating their own successful businesses from home.

As Bill reads his *Allowing Statement*, he relaxes, lessens doubt and begins to feel hope about the *Law of Attraction* bringing his desire for financial freedom.

How to Create Your Own Allowing Statement

When it comes to your ideal desires, do you find yourself saying, "I can't have this *because*..." or, "I want such and such *but*...?"

Whenever you hear yourself using words like *but* or *because*, you have doubts and limiting beliefs about the desires you want to manifest.

As we've learned, one way to help lessen or remove doubts and limited beliefs is by writing an *Allowing Statement*.

Start by reading your *Statement of Desire* and use it to uncover any resistance. For example let's say your *Statement of Desire* says something like, "Thank you! I'm in the process of attracting my ideal weight," and the computer virus in your subconscious says, "*but* I'll probably gain it back quickly *because* weight is hard to keep off once you get older." Did you notice how that little voice in our head said two words pointing to limiting beliefs about our *Statement of Desire*? We've just uncovered some doubt.

Next, ask these questions to yourself.

- Is there anyone doing what you want?

- Does anyone have what you want?

- How many people are doing or having what you want today?

- How many people have done what you want?

It is important not to include yourself in your *Allowing Statement*. Always use the 3rd person to alleviate doubt. Making a reference to yourself often creates more doubt. Make sure the *Allowing Statement* you create is plausible.

Allowing Statement

Millions of people are losing weight everyday. Thousands of people my age have lost weight and kept it off. Hundreds of people on this planet are enjoying healthy bodies every day. At this very moment, lots of people my age have lost weight and have kept the pounds off for years.

Allowing Statements can remove doubt and help with Step #3 of the *Deliberate Manifestation* process, *Allowing*.

More on Limited Beliefs

Are your beliefs based on your experiences, or do you experience what you believe? That sounds like a trick question.

If you believe that your experiences shape your belief system (most of us do), you give up your power and live your life on auto-pilot taking what comes your way, dealing with it as a victim of circumstances and most likely, complaining and focusing on it in such a way that the *Law of Attraction* can only bring you more to complain about!

On the other hand, if you believe you experience what you believe, you can realize what a powerful tool you have to experience what you desire. You simply need to *change* your beliefs. This way you actually create your life and set the forces in motion to attract what you want to experience.

The beliefs we have are formed in 3 ways:

1. Deliberately created, i.e. "I choose to believe I am abundant."
2. Taught to us by authority figures, i.e. Joe's father told him life was difficult and he would have to struggle without a college education.
3. The opposite of someone else's belief, i.e. Sally's mother told her women need a man to take care of them in this cruel world and Sally resists this belief

and creates her own million-dollar business just to prove her mother wrong.

The question we need to ask ourselves is, "Do we want to hold someone else's beliefs that are not serving us, or take back our power and create our own beliefs?"

Your life is a result of your beliefs. Everything you think and say is a belief. Everything is a belief and you have the power to change anything you want just by changing your beliefs. You can change anything, be anything, and do anything you choose.

A Belief We Must Believe

"The Law of Attraction gives us exactly what we expect to receive. What we expect to receive is formed by what we believe we will receive."

If we believe we are sick, overweight, un-loved, financially strapped, unattractive, or whatever, the *Law of Attraction* will deliver the same.

Have you ever said statement like these?

- I just can't get ahead.
- I'm so sick of struggling.
- I just need some relief.
- Every relationship goes bad for me.

- If it weren't for bad luck I'd have no luck at all.
- This is too good to be true.

When you use statements like these you're placing your order with the *Universe* and the vibrations you're sending cause the *Law of Attraction* to deliver exactly what you've stated. Not deliberately, mind you, but the subconscious mind holds these expectations and limiting beliefs and they become unconscious habits ready and waiting to sabotage the life you want to create.

How can we change our expectations? Deliberately of course! Deliberately expect the best. Instead of expecting a mailbox full of bills, expect to see a check. When your boss asks to see you privately, don't expect to get fired, expect a raise and a promotion!

Several times during the course of your day, stop and expect something wonderful. The more you focus on great expectations, the more often the *Law of Attraction* will send you the results.

> *Life is like music. There's the melody and the lyrics. The lyric is the story you write. The melody is the energy you work with.*

Getting It

In this chapter we learned how to create *Allowing Statements*.

- Noticing and changing limited beliefs can help remove doubt and change our expectations.

- When we use the words **but** and **because**, it's a good indication that we are holding limiting beliefs.

- Limited beliefs can be changed by asking questions like, "Is there anyone on the planet doing (blank) today?"

- The **Law of Attraction** gives us exactly what we expect to receive. What we expect to receive is formed by what we **believe** we will receive.

Chapter Eight

The 'Why' behind the Asking

It's really easy to ask the universe for what you want, but it's not always easy to receive what you ask for.

We've learned the most important part of the *Deliberate Manifestation* process is Step #3, *Allowing*, so let's back up to Step #1 where we are identifying our desires and getting ready to ask for them and see how this step may have hindered our progress.

We've used our *What Do I Want* worksheet to briefly observe what we don't want and re-frame those items to what we do want. So, stop for a moment and get out your worksheet, look at it and see how you're *feeling* when you read what you've written on the *Feels Good* side.

When you look at your *Do Wants* do you feel any fear or worry? Any fear or worry you're feeling can be negative blocks, limited beliefs you have, and lack of trust and faith in the universe. Knowing what we've learned about thoughts and feelings, any fears and resistance surfacing here are conflicting vibrations.

When you use the words *'or else'*, it's a good indication your desire is based in fear. Let's say our desire pertains to money. We're clear we want more money to pay bills, buy a car, have a nicer life-style, etc. So our thought is, "I desire more money," but our feeling is, *"or else* I can't pay my mortgage."

You need to be aware of what is fueling your desire for money. What is the emotion behind the asking? Most people are asking for what they *don't have*, so they're coming from a negative space of lack and limitation. The most we can expect to manifest is nothing, or more of what we *don't have*.

The *Deliberate Manifestation* process requires that we monitor our thoughts and feelings to ensure that the vibrations we're sending and including in our *Vibrational Aura* are in alignment with what we're asking for.

When you ask, "I want to attract more money," and the little voice inside you says, "How is this going to happen?" you're vibrations are not in alignment and you're not allowing the manifestation.

This is only natural because we want to make sense of the attraction process, however, we can't allow a thought like, "How is this going to happen?" to become our dominant vibration.

- How will I attract more money?
- How will I find true love?

- How can I lose this weight?
- How can I find a job that allows me to be creative?

When we have the feeling that we must **do** something in order for the **Law of Attraction** to work, we have doubts about the whole process. When we're thinking and feeling **how**, the vibration we're really sending out sounds like:

- I don't think this **Law of Attraction** thing will work.
- I have some strong doubts about this stuff.
- It may have worked for some people but not for me.

When you ask **how** over and over again you still believe you must **do** something to make it happen. What you need to **do** is keep your vibration positive. That feeling of **how** will just bring you more of **how**!

Notice how you feel when you think **how**. The positive vibration and feeling you had about your desires change immediately from feeling good to feeling bad. This is where you need to be deliberate and stop your **how thinking** back to **allow thinking** and change your vibration. Become aware of words that stop you from feeling good about your wants and desires. When that little voice is saying **how**, recognize what's happening and in that very moment change your thought to what makes you feel good.

Allowing is similar to a leap of faith; faith in the **Universe**. When a farmer plants a seed he knows it will grow. He doesn't go out to his field every morning and dig up his seed to see if it's germinating. He's confident the seed will grow and he waters it every day. He *allows* the process.

Plant your seeds of desire and let the *Universe* make it grow. *Allow* yourself to dwell in your imagination, free to enjoy whatever it is you want to create without worry or fear of how to get it to manifest.

"I now *allow* myself the manifestation of…"

Getting It

Let's recap what we've learned.

- When our desire is based in fear we are not in alignment. We are not allowing the process.

- Using the words, *'or else'* is a good indication of a fear-based desire.

- If the emotion behind the asking is lack and limitation we can only expect the same to return to us.

- When we feel we have to *do* something, we are not trusting in the *Law of Attraction* process.

- Allowing is having faith in the *Universe* and that we will receive what we ask for.

Chapter Nine

Attracting Abundance

Question: If you wanted to attract more ideal clients, what vibration do you need to be offering?

Answer: To attract more ideal clients, you need to be offering the vibration of ideal clients.

To attract more available parking spaces, you need to be offering the vibration of available parking spaces.

To attract clear skies and the rain stopping so you don't get your new hairdo wet, you need to be offering the vibration of clear skies.

To attract more abundance into your life, you need to be offering the vibration of more abundance.

There's a secret here. The vibration you offer is a *feeling*. No matter if it's ideal clients, available parking spaces, better health, soul mate, or whatever… it's a feeling.

Abundance isn't a thing, it's a feeling.

For example, let's say you're expecting an income tax refund check. You know you've done everything right and when you calculated it, it came to over $3,000.

Do you feel abundant knowing the refund check is?

1. Coming in the mail
2. When you have the check in your hand, or
3. When you deposit the money in the bank?

Answer: When you know the check is coming!

"Wow, I've got a nice big check coming. I'm *feeling* so excited. I'm going to buy this and this and this!"

Abundance has nothing to do with money in the bank. It has nothing to do with money in your hand. But, it has everything to do with your feelings. Abundance is a feeling.

To be a deliberate attractor, feelings need to be *deliberate*. As deliberate attractors we need to deliberately offer the vibration of what it is we want. In order to attract more abundance, we need to be offering the vibration of abundance. That's why its good news to know it's a feeling.

The Feelings Game

If we invented a board game complete with little cards and I picked up a card and it said **ANGER**, I could offer the vibration of anger.

If I picked up another card that said **JOY**, I could offer the vibration of joy.

You and I can vibrate *every* feeling in the whole world. You can deliberately vibrate that feeling. You can deliberately create every feeling.

The next card is **HURT**. "Ok, I can vibrate that too."

"Oh, look at me! I got the **ABUNDANCE** card."

Can we offer the vibration of abundance on purpose? *Yes!*

Tools for Offering Deliberate Vibrations

- Observe and Celebrate

- Record Evidence

- Abundance Games

Abundance is a feeling. You understand that you can deliberately offer *any* vibration (feeling). To attract more abundance, you simply need to offer the vibration of *abundance*.

If someone unfamiliar with the ***Law of Attraction*** was asked the question, "How much time a day do you offer the vibration of abundance?" the answer would be zero.

Most people don't offer the vibration of abundance at all. How can the ***Law of Attraction*** bring you something you're not focused on? How can the ***Law of Attraction*** check if you're not holding the vibration to be matched?

If I asked somebody on the street the question, "What could you do to attract more money this month?" most people would answer; Get a job, buy lottery tickets, sell something on eBay, get a part-time job, work overtime, etc. These are the most common answers. But, there are many other abundant things we can discover as deliberate attractors.

Tool #1: Observe and Celebrate

From now on until the rest of your life, in the very moment that you deem something is abundant to you, *celebrate it*!

I had a job once where I worked for a neighbor that lived across the street. Instead of taking my car to work everyday, I was able to ride with him and save $30.00 a week in gas. I was abundant with free transportation. I was excited. I celebrated my abundance. It was like making an extra $120.00 a month!

Some of you know I'm also a musician. When I lived in New York and played music at different pubs, part of the deal was a free dinner every night I played. If you've ever been to New York, most dinners at a pub are in the $15-$20 range and this amounted to an extra $100.00 or more abundance every week!

What are some things you could deem abundant? Free website resources, free eBooks, discounts on memberships, coupons, air miles, free parking, a 2nd cup of coffee, finding money, free advice, barter and trades are some other things we can call abundance.

It's not the monetary value of these things; it's the fact that you attracted these abundant things. Notice how that *feels*?

You need to notice and celebrate the abundance that you attract (feel it) so you can attract even more. Keep adding more things to your *Vibrational Aura* by noticing whenever you're attracting abundance. Celebrate it at that very moment.

Remember whatever vibration is captured in your *Vibrational Aura* is the one the *Law of Attraction* responds to. So, if you can be more deliberate and celebrate all the abundance you receive and the abundance all around you, you would offer the vibration of abundance and receive more.

A wise man hears one word and understands two.

Isn't it better noticing 3 things today, spending 10 minutes celebrating it and deliberately offering the abundance vibration than not noticing and spending zero minutes?

A most popular question people are always asking me is, "How do I stay connected? What do I do to stay deliberate? I have binders and notebooks full of *What I Want* worksheets and I can't stay connected!"

Most of your work with the *Law of Attraction* is celebrating or being grateful. I like to say, "You can stay connected by having an *Attitude of Gratitude*."

"I love this! Thank you!" Keep noticing and celebrating. Find the abundance you already have in your life and be thankful for it because that positive attitude becomes the positive vibration in your *Vibrational Aura* and the *Law of Attraction* can only bring you more of it!

Write down everything that is a close match in your journal every night. What is in your vibration? There's a reason it's called deliberate attraction. We need to be deliberate in our offering of vibrations. Writing in your journal every night for 10 minutes deliberately offers the vibration you're celebrating.

Observe abundance, feel abundance, celebrate abundance and observe some more abundance. It's a cycle of observe, feel, celebrate, observe, feel, celebrate over and over again.

Find something to make your vibrations higher when faced with negativity. Think about your grand kids, or your puppy. Find something to celebrate and be grateful for.

Doesn't that *feel* good?

The Seeing Things That Are Abundant Game

Play this game when you're not feeling very abundant.

Look out the window and notice all the leaves on the trees. Notice all the birds and squirrels. Notice all the wonderful grass. Notice the beautiful blue skies or the millions of stars in the sky. Inside the house, notice all your things. Notice your books, your computer, your clothes, and your music collection. Make up your own list of abundance in your life and the abundance all around you. Keep noticing and keep vibrating abundance and gratitude.

In the excitement (feeling) of noticing all the abundance around you, you offer more abundance in your vibrational aura. Get yourself into a state of appreciation and recap everything you've attracted this week. It's really a simple formula. Notice the positive and the *Law of Attraction* will match it and bring you more and more.

The Lottery Ticket Trick

When people buy those scratch-off lottery tickets and they win $2.00 right there, 9 times out of 10 they will cash it in.

By doing this, they only have the vibration of abundance for a brief moment.

They were all pumped-up for a minute or two and they briefly offered the vibration of abundance and then they buy another ticket and win again.

They cash that ticket in and they keep playing the game until they lose. On the way home they're telling themselves, "I just lost $4.00," and then they spend twenty minutes beating themselves up saying, "I'll never do that again!"

When you win your $2.00 lottery ticket, don't cash it in! That winning lottery ticket is worth more to you vibrationally than it is cashed in.

I've probably got eight winning lottery tickets in my wallet right now. Financially that's worth $16.00 but vibrationally, it's priceless.

What's something I can tell myself when I open up my wallet and I see all those winning lottery tickets? What are some truthful things I can say about that?

"I won the lottery 8 times! I'm so abundant! Look at how lucky I am! I'm a winner of lottery tickets! When I open my wallet and I see 8 winning lottery tickets, I'm offering a vibration of abundance by celebrating it.

When somebody says, "Why are you carrying all those winning tickets?" I say, "Well, I won the lottery eight times!" So they say, "Why don't you cash them in?" And I tell them, "Because, I like telling you the story that I won the lottery eight times. In fact, I'll do anything to tell you the story that I won the lottery eight times!"

The lottery tickets are worth $16.00 in cash or they can be priceless in raising your abundance vibration.

The Check Game

Make this a regular habit. Whenever you receive a check in the mail, carry it around with you for a while. Most people don't hold on to the checks they receive for very long at all. Usually people will deposit the check in the bank the same day the receive it, but if you don't have to, hold on to the check for a few days and raise your abundance vibration. You really don't have to cash it the day you receive it.

What if you had two or three checks in your wallet for a few days and every time you opened your wallet you had winning lottery tickets and un-cashed checks in there. Wouldn't you feel abundant every time you opened your wallet?

Then I would open my wallet lots more, wouldn't I?

The quickest way to double your money is to fold it over and put it back in your pocket.

More Ways to Trick the Universe

- Add some zeros to the balance on your bank statement.

- Carry a fifty or a hundred dollar bill in your wallet.

Jack Canfield, the author of the *Chicken Soup for the Soul* books, took a one dollar bill and added five zeros to it making it a One Hundred Thousand dollar bill. He then taped it to the ceiling above his bed and every morning when he woke up he saw the bill and a year later he manifested $100,000.00.

Seeing it and observing it will change the vibration.

$10,000 a Day Exercise

This is a great exercise to get your vibrations set to abundance. Pretend your shopping and spend $10,000 a day for 7 days. Ideally, you would buy many things that added up to $10,000.

The purpose of this exercise is to help you include things in your vibrational aura. These can be material things or whatever you would want to do with the money.

Most people don't include the things they want in their vibration. In fact, some people will pick up a catalog and not even look at it because they believe they can't afford anything. They never get to include the things they desire in their vibration.

Get a little journal and start writing in it each night. "Wow $10,000, what am I going to buy today?"

You don't spend it all in one sitting. Maybe you go downtown and say, "You know what? I'm buying that tonight." By telling yourself you're buying that or you want that, you've just included that in your vibration. Then you see something else and say, "Wow! I'd love to get that tonight! You know, tonight I'm going to book myself a massage!"

What this exercise allows you to do, or invites you and encourages you to do, is to include all these things in your *Vibrational Aura* without having money in the equation. At night time you write in your journal, "Ok, I'm going to buy $500 worth of that. I'm going to spend $1000 here."

People might say, "Why $10,000? Why not a million?" Some of you would disagree, but most people wouldn't know how to spend a million dollars if they had it, especially if they had a million dollars to spend every day for seven days. Most people will have trouble spending $10,000 a day for seven days.

These exercises are games and the *Law of Attraction* doesn't care if it's a game, a fantasy, your imagination, or real. It's just picking up on your vibration and matching it.

Getting It

In this chapter we learned about abundance.

- When we are talking about abundance we're not necessarily talking about money.

- Abundance is a *feeling*.

- We can offer any feeling we want; love, hate, joy and abundance.

- Learn to observe all the abundance that you have and all the abundance around you. By doing so, you are including the vibration of abundance in your *Vibrational Aura*.

Chapter Ten

The Law of Attraction and Money

Money, money, money! The number one question I receive from people all over the world; *"How can I attract more money into my life using the Law of Attraction?"*

Let's start by removing some limiting beliefs that 97% of the population shares.

- There's only so much money to go around.

- You must suffer to succeed.

- You have to work hard.

- Rich people are evil.

- Money is bad.

- It is spiritually noble to be poor.

Can you think of any other beliefs you have about money?

Let me tell you right now, they're all lies! When it comes to money (and most other things) we've been spoon-fed a set of limiting beliefs about cash-flow and abundance. We can thank our parents and their parents, our religions, our governments, the media and anyone or any thing else we let influence our belief system.

You were born to be healthy, happy and rich. Our Creator, the Source, All-That-Is, whatever you would like to call this Magnificent Energy, desires your prosperity and success. It doesn't want you to be poor, or to suffer, or experience limitation of any kind. The universe is abundant. Take a look! Abundance is everywhere. The universe is blessed with abundance and the Source wants you to be blessed. It wants you to have all the wealth and abundance you desire.

The Creator-God-Source is energy. Everything is energy. You are energy. You are a part of Source Energy and nothing can sever this connection. In this sense you are a child of God. Merely align yourself with the universe (by you thoughts) and you will have all the abundance you desire. Think prosperity and you are prosperous. It's all about vibrations and vibrating abundance.

The *Law of Attraction* is always working. You do not attract what you wish for, you attract what you expect. What you have now is a reflection of your beliefs and how you think. Think lack and limitation and you will attract lack and limitation.

The choice is always yours to make. You have the power to be, do and have more abundance and anything you desire.

Whatever you can imagine you can have by abundant thought, belief, desire and intent. Life is meant to be joyful and happy. Become a blessing and you will be blessed. You have the choice to think of life as a blessing, curse, drama, comedy, tragedy, adventure or whichever way you want. It's your decision.

Think abundant thoughts and desire abundant results. See it as real and be thankful. Enjoy having it. Believe in wealth and your right to it. Stop believing there is lack and limitation. There are none. When you think you have nothing, you have an abundance of nothing.

See yourself as wealthy and you will be wealthy. When you think about the word *money*, how do you feel? Are you full of any negative emotions like fear, tension, or disgust? Do you have fear that you won't be able to meet your bill payments, or that your business won't generate enough income to cover your expenses?

Do you feel like you don't have enough money and the things you want can't be had because there is never enough cash-flow? You are focused on lack and the *Law of Attraction* will bring you more of what you're focusing on! Focusing on lack can also lead to believing there's not enough business for you, like clients and customers. This can lead to resenting your competition.

Stop thinking of money as the enemy or as something you are constantly chasing. Start thinking of money as something you can enjoy. Money is simply a means to exchange energy.

Stop thinking about a lack of money and think about the money you do have, not the money you wish you had. When you're feeling stressed about money and focusing on all the bills that need to be paid, change your thought to what you have now and be grateful for it.

There is unlimited abundance and it's yours for the taking by changing your thought. When you start thinking abundance and prosperity, you will feel empowered and the *Law of Attraction* will bring you the people, events, opportunities and ideas to become more abundant.

The ancient beliefs that have been handed down to us through the ages are *money is evil* and *you can't be spiritual and have money*. Just look at Jesus. He was barefoot and poor his whole life. I'm sure you have heard that it is not spiritual to want money and spiritual information should be given for free.

This kind of thinking sends vibrational messages that will come back and keep us from creating cash-flow in our lives. Money is a form of energy and energy has no beginning and no end. There is an abundance of energy for everyone.

If you want your money situation to change, you have to change the shape and image of it in your mind first. Then, you must increase your ability to allow the energy to move freely by eliminating tension and resistance (negative beliefs and feelings) going on within you. If you don't have an image of cash-flow in the vibrations you're sending out, how can you attract it? You must first see that it exists in your mind and include it in your *Vibrational Aura*. If we want things to change in our outer reality, we must first change things in our inner reality.

> *The only reason anyone doesn't have enough money is because they are blocking money from coming to them by the vibrational thought they're holding.*

Every negative thought and belief (how you feel about money) is blocking cash from flowing to you. You must change your thoughts from lack of money to more than enough money. If you feel you **need** money, you will continue to attract the need for money. You must **know** without a doubt that the universe will provide for you.

Remember it's not your job to figure out **how** the money will come to you, just ask for it, believe you will receive it, and feel happy about it.

If you have the feeling that the only way money will come to you is through your current job, immediately let that thought go because as you continue to think that limited thought you will get your wish. If you see something you want and you think, "I can't afford that," you will get your wish.

From this moment on when you see something that you would like to have, change your thought to, "I can afford that." And, "I can buy that." This self-talk will cause a shift in your emotions and you will begin to feel better about money, and as you convince yourself that you can afford those things, you will get your wish.

Giving is a powerful tool to receive money. When you give money away making donations or helping a beggar on the street, your vibration is of abundance and the feeling is, "I have more money than I need." As you give the *Law of Attraction* matches the vibration and gives you more of it. If you think you don't have enough money to give, ignore that thought and start giving…with gratitude. The universe will give you even more money to give away!

Abundance is your birthright and your thoughts will give you more abundance in every area of your life.

Getting It

Let's recap what we learned about the *Law of Attraction* and money.

- It is impossible to bring more money into your life when you give your attention, energy and focus to the lack of it.

- Use 'self-talk' to create a mind set of wealth and abundance. As you feel better about money, more will come to you.

- Stop saying, "I can't afford it." Begin to feel better about money by saying, "I can buy that" or "I can afford this."

- Give money to charities, the homeless, or any cause you deem appropriate, with gratitude which feels good. Don't sacrifice to give, which feels bad. When you're being generous with your money you're including, "I have plenty" in your *Vibrational Aura*.

- Think wealth and abundance… always.

You may be disappointed if you fail, but you are doomed if you don't try.

Chapter Eleven

The Law of Attraction and Relationships

Relationships are the key to being successful and living life to the fullest. Humans are not meant to be alone. We're meant to connect with others.

When I use the word, *relationship*, I'm including romantic relationships, parents, children, relatives, children, co-workers, friends and everyone else you come in contact with.

If you want better relationships, be a better relationship for others. How you are, and the way you think and feel will attract the same qualities back to you. It's all about vibrations and how you're vibrating.

There are only two kinds of emotions, love and fear. Every other emotion will fall under either of these.

What does this have to do with the *Law of Attraction* and relationships? Everything! If your vibration is love, you'll attract more love and positive people. If your vibration is fear, more negative emotion and negative people will cross your path.

We attract our significant others by how we feel about ourselves. When we don't feel secure and confident, we will only feel comfortable with people who are vibrating a similar way. It might not feel good to be around this type of person, but it feels *normal* to you. When you meet someone who is vibrating higher than you, you may not feel you're good enough to date them.

Before the *Law of Attraction* can bring you high-quality people into your life, you must feel that you are a person who is of high-quality. As your vibrational frequency changes, the people who come into your life, romantic or otherwise, will be at a similar vibrational frequency.

"My life's falling apart. My boyfriend left me and I keep attracting men who blah, blah, blah."

The answer is always the same. *You always get what you vibrate*.

When your friend, Mary, comes up to you and says she keeps attracting men that do this and this and this, you're thinking, "Mary, you're getting what you vibrate."

And, your other friend says to you, "My business is failing. I keep getting clients that don't have money." The answer is the same. He's getting what he's vibrating.

No matter what the scenario is, the answer is always the same. You always get what you vibrate.

But, that's a short answer to give somebody, isn't it? We need to be gentler and stay in rapport with everybody. We need to uncover where it was that our friends were offering that vibration. Of course, this applies to us as well. Where are we offering the vibration that generates results we don't want and how can we deliberately change?

The best approach is to teach our friends what the *Law of Attraction* is, how everyone attracts what they vibrate, and then help them identify what it was that they were doing that offered the negative vibration. We need to show them how to be more deliberate in their offering.

It's a Frequency Thing

Imagine we just drew a radio dial with a frequency range going from 0-100.

<< Relationships Frequency Dial >>

0_____Mary_____50_____Me___100

The word *frequency* is similar to vibration.

Here you are sitting around having a wonderful day. The birds are singing. The sky is blue and the sun is shining.

You're receiving great phone calls from friends and family. It's a great day all around! Let's say you're 97.6 on the radio dial. You attract all sorts of great things quickly or over night. You attract everything at 97.6. We love being at 97.6!

Oh, but it's not all wonderful. You've just noticed that you're by yourself and not everybody in your life is vibrating at 97.6.

Let me tell you about my friend Mary. Mary is not at 97.6. She's at 29.2. In other words, she's got very negative vibes. I'm going to put Mary on the radio dial above at 29.2.

The difference from Mary's 29.2 to my 97.6 is indicating lots of distance, isn't it? We can also call that distance, *resistance*. I'm at 97.6 and Mary is at 29.2.

Sometimes you'll meet somebody and after the meeting you'll say, "Wow, did I ever like them! They were so cool. I really like them." What you really mean is, "Wow, we're on the same frequency."

You can tell when someone is offering the same vibration as you are. You can tell by how you *feel*. You'll feel good!

Sometimes you meet somebody and two minutes later you're thinking, "Oh my God! I think he's a real jerk! I don't match with him at all. This feels horrible. I don't like him! I don't even know his name and I don't like him."

Now you understand that you and this person weren't on the same vibration. Their vibration was lower. The same applies to when you're with someone who makes you feel really good. They're raising your vibration to meet theirs!

This distance between mine and Mary's vibrations is called *resistance*. The distance between my vibration and someone else's vibration is equal to how much resistance I *feel* when I'm with them. If I'm on 97.6 and you're on 92.3, there is very little resistance

So why would you hang around with a negative person like Mary? Well, there's a reason. Mary is my mother, my wife, my sister, etc. Some people just have to be in your life.

You can help the situation by ***minding your vibration***. By maintaining it, looking after it, and being deliberate about it.

If you're vibration is 97.6 and you're having a really great day and Mary calls, you need to know how to mind your vibration and keep it at 97.6 because after you talk to Mary and hang up the phone, if you don't maintain your high vibration you'll feel lousy and get in a negative funk.

After your conversation with your negative friend, your vibration won't automatically spring back up to 97.6. You stay in that funk. You're thinking, "Did she ever tick me off!" You stay in that negative space.

Remember the car radios from the old days when you pushed the button to *lock* in the radio station you liked? I'm going to teach you a technique to lock in your vibration, or how to *mind* it.

Mind Your Vibrations

The next time you're talking to someone and they're complaining about what they don't want, what they don't like about something, and how they don't like this and how they don't like that, you have two choices.

One choice is to buy-in and feed the conversation, swimming around in the muck with them and joining them in their negative vibes. The other choice is to simply ask them, *"So, what do you want?"*

How do you mind your vibration?

- You mind it by managing and controlling the kinds of conversations you have.

- You only choose food that you like on the buffet.

- You only sleep in beds that are comfortable.

- You only smell things that feel good.

- You only have conversations that bring you joy.

Your goal is to only do and experience things and people that bring you joy and happiness. That's all! Feel good and the *Law of Attraction* sends you more to feel good about.

Your negative friend might not like the change in you and they will find someone else to complain to, someone vibrating at their negative frequency.

And what is it that you're really doing? You're teaching people how you want to be treated, because people will treat you the way you allow them to!

One time I was having a conversation with my friend Mary and I kept saying, "What do you want? What do you want?" Well, I know I made her mad, I could just tell.

Mary wouldn't talk to me for a couple of weeks, but when she did call, what do you suppose she told herself before she phoned? Right! I didn't hear any negativity and we had a very pleasant phone call. She knew I wouldn't buy into her negativity and I wouldn't go down that funky road. I trained her how to treat me.

Ideally, people should be on the same vibrational frequency if they decide to marry. You're going to want to marry somebody you're in vibrational harmony with and of course, we know some couples aren't in vibrational harmony at all.

Let's say a couple gets married and they're both on vibrational radio dial 50.3. Are they in vibrational harmony and happy with each other? Yes! They're on 50.3. They don't even know about 97.6. They're doing fine vibrating at 50.3. They're very compatible.

Now, one of those people decides to learn the *Law of Attraction* and takes other personal development courses and so on. They have now raised their vibration from 50.3 to 90.7. The vibes they have now are very different from their spouse's 50.3.

When one of the partners raises their vibrations and locks it in, they just created *resistance*. They've created distance in the vibrations.

Do you treat yourself the way you want other people to treat you? When you don't treat yourself the way you want to be treated, you can never change the way things are. If you do not treat yourself with love and respect, you are in fact offering the vibration that you aren't important enough or deserving of anything better than what you have now.

The *Law of Attraction* will obediently send you more people who don't love and respect you. You need to treat yourself with love and respect and then the *Law of Attraction* will fill your life with people who love and respect you. You'll find filling yourself up with love until you're overflowing will give you more than enough love to give to others.

Many of us were taught to put others first. Unless you fill yourself up first, you will have nothing to give to anybody. People are responsible for their own happiness. When you follow your bliss and do what makes you joyful and happy, you don't have to think about giving. It's just naturally overflows to others.

Love yourself first because it's impossible to feel good if you don't love yourself. When you feel bad about yourself, you're repelling all the love and goodness the universe is sending you. When you feel bad about yourself, your vibrational frequency is attracting more people and situations to make you feel bad about yourself.

Begin to celebrate and be grateful for all the things that are wonderful about you. As you focus on those things, the *Law of Attraction* will show you more wonderful things about you.

Your Current Relationships

When it comes to our current relationships, be it with our spouse, partner, children, relatives, friends and associates, we tend to focus on what we don't like about them. We're always complaining, "My wife is such a nag. My kids won't behave. My boss is an idiot." We're focused on what we don't like or what we want to change in the other person. We need to focus on (notice and celebrate) what we appreciate about the other people in our life, not what we don't like about them. When we're complaining about those things, we just get more of it.

Even if you're involved in a really bad relationship; you're not getting along, things aren't working and you're fighting all the time. You can still change things. You can deliberately attract what you want by writing down all the things you like about the person and the things you appreciate about them. You can write down all the reasons you fell in love with them in the first place. When you focus on what you like and appreciate about them, and put that in your *Vibrational Aura*, the *Law of Attraction* will bring you more of that and the problems will disappear.

No one can create your happiness. You are the person in charge of your feelings of joy and happiness. Others can only share in your happiness. Your joy is inside you.

Joy, happiness, and love are feelings… a state of being. Love everything you can. Love everyone you can. Focus on love and you will experience that love coming back to you. The universe will bring you more of everything… and more people to love.

Getting It

Let's go over what we learned.

- If you want better relationships, be a better relationship for others.

- We attract others by how we feel about ourselves.

- If your vibrations are at a high frequency you will attract people of a similar vibration.

- The difference in the frequency of two people is called resistance.

- We learned to maintain our vibrations by staying away from things and people that make us feel bad.

- Love yourself first and you will overflow with love to give to others.

- No one can create your happiness. Only you.

The best thing a father can do for his children is to love their mother.

Chapter Twelve

The Law of Attraction and Health

Science and the medical profession are beginning to realize our thoughts, feelings and emotions determine our state of health.

We've all heard stories of patients receiving a placebo sugar pill and being told the placebo will have a beneficial effect for such and such malady. More often than not, the power of the patient's mind combined with the sugar pill creates the desired results, sometimes more so than prescribed medication.

The placebo effect is a powerful phenomenon proving that when someone thinks and believes the sugar pill is a cure, they will receive what they believe.

Healing with your mind can work in tandem with traditional medicine. Medication can alleviate the pain which will allow the person to focus their thoughts on perfect health and the *Law of Attraction* will bring about the desired results.

Focusing your thoughts on perfect health is the same as focusing your thoughts on financial freedom, a loving relationship or the perfect career. The *Deliberate Manifestation* process is the same for *all* areas of your life. We use the same steps, tools and techniques to manifest health as we do to manifest wealth.

"What I Want Worksheet"	
Name: Millie	
My Ideal Healthy Body	
FEELS BAD	**FEELS GOOD**
Always tired	Feel vibrant and energetic
Look too fat	Look thin and trim
Gets out of breath	Breathe easily
Feels bad all the time	Feel good all the time
Uncontrollable eating	Controlled eating habits
Dislikes exercise	Enjoys nature walking
Hates boring health food	Loves interesting healthy food
Looks bad in clothes	Looks great in clothes
Low self-esteem	Confident, loves self
Gets sick or worse	Healthy, happy body
>>>>> This is what I want >>>>>	

My friend, Millie, wanted to loose weight. In fact, she had let herself balloon up to 250 pounds. She was always complaining about how she was tired and didn't feel good.

I had Millie start with a ***What Do I Want*** worksheet and list everything she didn't want on the ***Feels Bad*** side and then I had her reframe that list to ***Do-Wants*** on the ***Feels Good*** side. Keep in mind a minimum of 50-100 items should be listed for ideal clarity.

Millie is getting clear about what she wants and now she needs to give her desire attention, energy and focus.

Millie needs to uncover any negative blocks and limiting beliefs she may have concerning what she wants and any ***buts*** or ***because*** statements she hears from her inner voice as she reviews her worksheet.

- "I would like to loose weight, ***but*** my family has a history of having a hard time keeping it off."

- "I want a healthy body, ***but*** I've tried before and I can't control my sweet tooth."

- "I would like to exercise, ***but*** I don't want to get tired and work up a sweat."

- "I want to loose weight ***because*** I'm afraid I'll never get married looking like this."

As Millie determines the limited beliefs and negative blockages she has, she can write an *Allowing Statement* to help remove doubt.

- "Millions of people are enjoying a healthy lifestyle every day."

- "Thousands and thousands of people have lost weight and enjoy exercising by taking nature walks every day."

- "Just today, hundreds of people have learned to control their sweet tooth and enjoy eating healthy foods."

Now Millie can put everything together, remove doubt, and put her attention energy and focus on her desire to achieve an ideal healthy body.

Opening Statement

"Thank you. I'm in the process of attracting all I need to do, know and have to attract my ideal healthy body."

Item Statements

"I love knowing that an ideal healthy body makes me look wonderful in clothes. I'm excited at the thought of taking walks and breathing easily while I enjoy nature. I love how it feels to know my ideal body makes me confident and healthy. I've decided my ideal healthy body is vibrant, and looks thin and trim."

Closing Statement

"The Law of Attraction is matching my vibrational energy and doing what needs to be done to manifest my desire. I now allow myself the manifestation of an ideal healthy body."

The *Law of Attraction* will bring us what we focus on. If we focus on disease, our thoughts will attract more disease. Diseases can't exist in a body that's in a positive emotional state. Dis-ease means not at ease.

Our bodies come equipped with a basic health program called *self-healing*. If we cut ourselves, the wound will grow back together. If we get an infection, our immune system will fight the bacteria and make us well again. New cells are produced in our bodies every day while the old cells are discarded. Since science has proven this fact, the only reason a disease would stay in the body would be because it is held there by negative vibrations and our attention to illness, i.e. "I feel lousy today. I can't seem to shake this flu."

Illness cannot exist in a body that has a positive vibration. Think only positive thoughts and have a belief system that says health is our birthright and soon the *Law of Attraction* will bring us the perfection we seek.

You can see how our belief system about aging is all in our minds. Our beliefs tell us when we hit 40 it's all down hill and we'll be lucky if we live past 75 or so. *Aging* is a limited belief, so change the belief, renew your body and *know* you can think you way to optimum health.

If you have an illness, don't focus on it. Don't complain to your friends and family about it and worst of all, don't *own* it by saying things like, "I would go to the shopping mall if it wasn't for *my* anxiety." I would love to go to the game with you, but my doctor says I should take it easy because of *my* heart condition."

Try to have positive thoughts even when you're experiencing pain. Say something like, "Thank you for the healing I am attracting" and really mean it. When someone asks you how you feel, be thankful they reminded you to keep having positive thoughts of wellness.

Laughter attracts happiness and joy. It releases negative thoughts and feelings and attracts well-being. Disease is held in the body by thinking about it, observing it, and by giving attention to it. If you want to feel well, feel good and think good thoughts and the universe will grant your wish.

Getting It

Here is what we learned about the *Law of Attraction* and health.

- Our thoughts and feelings determine our state of health.

- Focusing on perfect health will attract perfect health.

- The only reason a disease would stay in the body would be because it is held there by our attention to the illness.

- When someone asks you how you feel, be thankful they reminded you to keep having positive thoughts of wellness.

Anxiety does not empty today of its sorrows, but only empties today of it's strength.

Chapter Thirteen

Getting Out of the Way

Did someone say this was easy? If you're not manifesting what you want, more often than not we are unconsciously creating blocks that cause a resistance. Here are some tools to help us get out of our own way.

Creating a Vacuum

How can you hold *it* in your hands if your hands are already holding something else? If you want to hold something new in your life, make sure nothing is already occupying the space.

A vacuum or void is an empty space waiting to be filled. For example, let's say you want more customers for the product you're selling. Make some space in your filing cabinet for the customers you want to attract. You can even label some folders with words like, *"Next Customer"* or *"New Client."* Doing this simple trick sets an intention that you want to attract more customers and the *"New Customer"* folder creates an empty space that is expected (allowed) to be filled. Feel the difference in vibrations when you say, "I need new customers to sell my product to" and "I have space for new customers." Which statement feels better?

In your appointment book you can enter *New Customer* here or *New Client Meeting* here at various times of the day. This creates a vacuum and an intention to attract what you want. When you open your agenda you will be reminded of your intention and you'll be giving it more energy and focus.

On the other hand when a client cancels an appointment, rather than complaining about it and getting in a negative space, instead change your vibration and see a new opportunity by thinking, "Great! I've just created space to attract a new customer."

Move the Energy

Get rid of what you don't want to make room for what you do want. If you haven't realized your manifestation, most likely you need to make room for it.

- Want new clothes? Make room in the closet.

- Want new furniture? Donate your old furniture to the Salvation Army.

- Want a girlfriend? Toss out any pictures you have of your old girlfriend.

To illustrate the point, there's a great story related by Mike Dooley, one of the teachers featured in **The Secret** movie. Mike's story told of a woman who had done all the right things trying to deliberately manifest her ideal partner. She had gotten clear about what she wanted in a romantic relationship and was giving her attention, energy and focus to her intention. However, her ideal man had yet to show up.

One day as she was parking her car in the middle of the garage she realized her actions were contradicting her desires. If her car was in the middle of the garage, she wasn't leaving any room for her ideal partner's car! Her actions were saying to the universe that deep down she didn't believe she would attract what she asked for.

She immediately created a vacuum by cleaning the garage and parking her car to one side leaving space for *his* car on the other side. Her closet was crammed full of her clothes, so she donated some to make space for *his* clothes. She was also sleeping in the middle of her bed, so she began sleeping on one side leaving space for her ideal partner.

After taking all these actions, creating a vacuum and acting as if she already received her perfect relationship, he arrived in her life and they are happily married.

Time, Patience and Faith

Is your manifestation here yet? No? You've done everything right and your ideal (blank) hasn't arrived? The answer may be *time*. It takes time for the energies we send out to the universe to come back to us.

Creation is instant. Time creates the illusion that our thoughts do not become instant manifestations. Passing time makes it seem like our creation is somehow separate from the energy that created it. Every positive or negative thought we have today is instantly manifested. It just hasn't arrived instantly because of what we call *time*.

Universal Timing is a time when everything is in sync. "To everything there is a season." The right time, the right place, and the right action all manifest when it is exactly *right* for everyone and everything on the planet and in the universe.

As you've learned, everything and everyone is energy. We are all connected. We are all *ONE*. Therefore, every thought and action affects not only us but everyone and everything. *Universal Timing* orchestrates the energy for the good of all. You may have your ideal set and giving it attention, but perhaps somewhere something is out of sync and not ready for the manifestation. When the *Universal Timing* is right, everything unfolds for your desire. What can help you cope with the delay? The answer is patience, acceptance and faith.

Patience, acceptance and faith are important elements in the process of *Deliberate Manifestation*. Everything you see around you was once just a thought in someone's head and mixed with enough patience, acceptance and faith to manifest in the third dimension. Many people have incredible ideas with very little faith to manifest them. You must give your ideas (ideals) attention, energy and focus to make them real, and have faith in the *Universe* and yourself to manifest them. Faith equals no doubt. The greatest creators in history, Thomas Edison, Albert Einstein, Henry Ford and Bill Gates among countless others, all shared an underlying conviction that their idea would become real. You are as powerful as you believe yourself to be.

Gratitude

Be thankful for what you have and the universe will bring you more to be thankful for. It is important to be grateful for what you have already manifested in your life. If you do nothing else in the *Deliberate Manifestation* process, being grateful will change your vibration to attract good into your life and more things to be grateful for!

A great way to be thankful for what you have is with a *Gratitude Journal*. Write down at least five things everyday that you are thankful for. You will discover things you are blessed with that you didn't even know you had. A change will happen deep inside you. You'll be delighted with how you feel about life. Being grateful is focusing on abundance and the *Law of Attraction* will bring you more abundance.

Appreciation helps you send out strong positive vibrations of pure happiness and joy. Writing in your *Gratitude Journal* is an effective tool for maintaining positive vibrations. When you purposely take the time to write down what you are thankful for, you are deliberately sending positive vibrations and including these in your *Vibrational Aura*.

You can be grateful for anything. The following was found on the Internet, author unknown.

Things I'm Thankful For

The partner who hogs the covers every night, because (s)he is not with someone else.

The child who is not cleaning his room, but is watching TV because that means he is at home and not on the streets.

For the taxes that I pay, because it means that I'm employed.

For the mess to clean after a party, because it means that I have been surrounded by friends.

For the clothes that fit a little too snug, because it means I have enough to eat.

For the shadow that watches me at work, because it means I am in the sunshine.

For the lawn that needs mowing, windows that need cleaning, and gutters that need fixing, because it means I have a home.

For all the complaints that I hear about the government, because it means that we have freedom of speech.

For the parking spot I find at the far end of the parking lot, because it means I am capable of walking and that I have been blessed with transportation.

For the huge heating bill, because it means I am warm.

For the lady in church who sings off key, because it means that I can hear.

For the pile of laundry and ironing, because it means I have clothes to wear.

For weariness and aching muscles at the end of the day, because it means I have been capable of working hard.

For the alarm that goes off in the early morning hours, because it means that I am alive.

For too much e-mail, because it means I have friends who are thinking of me.

You can be thankful for everything. You just need to see the positive. You can powerfully set your vibration and create your day with two simple words; *Thank You!* When you get out of the bed in the morning say; "Thank you for this brand new day." Say thank you as you brush your teeth and thank you as you take your shower. Say thank you as you eat your breakfast and say thank you for everything you're doing. Before you know it you have said thank you 100 times before you walk out the door!

As you start to feel different about what you have already, you will start to attract more good things.

You could be thinking, "I don't have a nice car. I don't have a good job or happy marriage," but this is only focusing on what you don't have. Be thankful for something as simple as having legs to walk and a mind to think with. The point is to stay grateful and positive so the *Law of Attraction* can bring you more to be grateful for. It is impossible to manifest great things in your life if you feel ungrateful for what you have. Negative feelings of resentment, jealousy, envy or dissatisfaction cannot bring you what you want unless you're looking for more things to be ungrateful for!

Remember, gratitude is part of your *Statement of Desire*;

> *"Thank you. I'm in the process of attracting all I need to do, know and have to attract my ideal (blank)."*

The Law of Forgiveness

Previously I was talking about creating a void or vacuum so you would have room for what you want to receive. Depending on what your intention and ideal is, donating clothes and things, moving your car to one side of the garage and sleeping on one side of the bed, etc. are great ways to create a vacuum. Giving up pain, resentment, jealousy, anger and fear is another way.

Just as donating your old clothes to make room for new clothes creates a void, negative emotions like the ones mentioned above must be eliminated in order to experience joy, peace, happiness and love.

I can't express how important forgiveness is. Most people have an area of their lives where energy is blocked because they have yet to forgive. This is especially true when it comes to relationships that went bad.

Most people have the wrong definition of forgiveness. They think that by forgiving a wrong done to them by another person that caused hurt and pain was somehow now okay. Forgiveness isn't about the other person. They don't even have to know about the forgiveness. Forgiveness is for you!

Forgiveness is actually one of the most positive gifts you can give. This includes forgiving others as well as yourself. When you forgive, you are releasing negative energy that is stuck and blocking the good that could be coming into your life.

You may think that after a relationship ended you were free of the other person forever. Actually any un-forgiveness you have only strengthens the bond between you and the other person. The negative energy is stagnant and keeping you from your positive ideal.

How do you know how to forgive? You'll know by how you *feel*. When you think of anyone from your past or present, if you feel any anger, resentment or hurt toward him or her, you need to activate the *Law of Forgiveness* and the energy will be immediately released. The breaking of this negative bond will miraculously affect the other person as well. If you are ever in contact with them again you may notice they are nicer and more pleasant now.

You must feel sincere when you forgive and most importantly, be *thankful*. Remember, you're not forgiving them for their action, you are *thanking* them *for-giving* you the opportunity to learn and grow from your interaction with them. What? Aren't you grateful to release all that negativity? Forgiveness does not mean approval. It means freedom!

Forgiveness is something you do for yourself.

When you forgive it will feel like you just removed a huge boulder from your shoulders.

It is just as important to forgive yourself. If you're angry with yourself for something, realize you are imperfect perfection and thank yourself *for-giving* yourself the opportunity to learn and grow, and to become a better person.

Getting It

Let's recap this chapter on getting out of the way.

- We may be unconsciously creating blocks that cause resistance to manifesting what we want.

- Creating a vacuum by removing people and things that do not serve our vibration will allow space for people and things that do.

- Creation is instant. *Universal Timing* is responsible for lining up the energy for the good of all people and things.

- Gratitude will cause the *Law of Attraction* to bring more to be grateful about.

- We can invoke the *Law of Forgiveness* to release negative energy in us. Forgiveness has nothing to do with the other person and everything to do with releasing blocked energy stopping the good from flowing to you.

The courageous person dies a single death; the fearful person dies a thousand times.

Chapter Fourteen

Tools for Emotional Clearing

We've learned that there is a simple *recipe* for attracting what you want in your life. As with any recipe, the *'cake'* will manifest by simply combining the correct ingredients and *allowing* the mixture to bake.

Manifesting or creating your life is as simple as following a recipe. Mix in a little 'what I want' with some attention, a pinch of energy and a dash of focus, and place it in the universal oven and presto, enjoy the tasty delights!

Oh, but you didn't start off with a clean bowl, did you? How can you expect anything good and tasty to happen if you mixed everything in a messy bowl?

The bowl is your *mind*. If your mind is a mess of stagnant negative energy like limiting beliefs, hurts, fears and doubts, whatever you're cooking (wanting to manifest) will either not show up or be totally different from what you wanted.

The following are some useful tools you can utilize for cleaning the 'bowl'.

Hypnosis and Meditation

Hypnosis, either from a certified hypnotherapist or by utilizing self-hypnosis and meditation, allows an individual to bypass his conscious mind and uncover stuck negative energies in the subconscious mind. When you use these techniques you will not be asleep. You will be in an altered state of consciousness where you will be able to access and remove blockages you may have causing resistance to the *Deliberate Attraction* process.

I have several hypnosis audios dealing with specific issues like manifesting, forgiving, and guided meditations available for purchase on my website (www.borntomanifest.com) which can help to release negativity in your subconscious. Do a search online for additional resources. Below is a script you're welcome to use if you would like to experiment with self-hypnosis.

Self-Hypnosis Script

Self-hypnosis allows an individual to program his/her subconscious mind with one or more suggestions that will help release emotional blockage much more easily than if working with just the conscious mind. When utilizing hypnosis you will not be asleep but in an altered state of consciousness whereby you will be aware of what is happening around you, but will have your concentration focused on one specific thing and you can invoke the *Law of Attraction* to uncover the issues for you.

During this process you will be in a "Theta" brain wave state in which you have a direct communication link between the conscious and subconscious minds, thus allowing you to program change directly into the subconscious.

The following 30 day program will assist you in developing the skills to enter the hypnotic state, and to invoke the *Law of Attraction*. You can uncover negative issues, release and then bring yourself back out. The best time to practice this technique is just prior to sleep or during another inactive period during the day. In order for you to master self-hypnosis you should practice the process for 21-30 consecutive days. If you miss more than 2 days in a row, the entire procedure should be started over.

4 Week Self-Hypnosis Instructions

Directions

- This program is best utilized with soft background music absent of lyrics.

- Get totally comfortable with the self-hypnosis procedure before trying to give yourself suggestions to bring about a habit pattern change.

Week 1

Get into a relaxed position where you will not be disturbed for approximately 30 minutes.

- Find an eye fixation point slightly above eye level and focus on it. Take a deep breath all the way in - hold - exhale slowly while relaxing and counting backward from 5 - 1. You will be taking 5 deep breaths during this process.

- Tell yourself your eyes are getting heavy. Finally, on the count of 1, if not before, allow your eyes to close; mood music can be utilized to enhance the experience. (Approximately 3 minutes)

- Relax yourself from the top of your head, down to the tips of your toes. (Approximately 4-8 minutes)

- When you are completely relaxed, mentally repeat the following suggestion: "Each time I utilize this process, I become more self-confident and more successful." (Approximately 1 minute)

- Count from 1-5; open your eyes, feeling relaxed, refreshed and rested. (Total process 10-25 minutes.) (If done at bedtime, count from 5-1 and end the process with your eyes closed.)

Week 2

- Repeat the same steps as week one, you should find the amount of time needed to reach the relaxed state becoming shorter.

- Between weeks 2 and 3, invoke the *Law of Attraction* to bring forth negative issues that need releasing; "Thank you! I am in the process of attracting and uncovering any negative blockages to my manifestations."

- Formulate a positive suggestion such as, "Thank you for my healing. I now release this stagnant energy concerning this issue," and write it on a 3x5 card. Use as few words as necessary. Use positive wording moving toward what you want to have happen, not away from the habit you want to change. At this point work on only one area of change at a time. (Total process 6-15 minutes)

Week 3

- Get into a comfortable position with the suggestion card in hand.

- Locate your focus spot, take your suggestion card, hold it between the focus point and your eyes, and read it to yourself 5 times.

- Drop the card, focus on the spot, take a deep breath, and start counting backward from 5-1.

- By the count of 1 if your eyes are not closed, close them. (After numerous repetitions, your eyes should become so heavy you will want to close them before the count of 1.)

- Relax your body quickly from the top of your head to the tip of your toes.

- Repeat the suggestion on the card over and over again for approximately 1 minute.

- For an additional minute repeat to yourself, "Each time I practice self-hypnosis, I achieve it faster and go deeper."

- Count from 1-5, open your eyes relaxed and refreshed or move into a sleep state. (Total process 4-10 minutes.)

Week 4

- Get into your comfortable position.

- Follow the steps from Week 3.

- Your body and mind should now be conditioned so you will automatically drift into a pleasant state of hypnosis. (Total process 2-4 minutes)

You may record your own hypnosis tape by utilizing relaxing music and writing your own adaptation of the script above.

Emotional Freedom Technique – EFT

Developed by Gary Craig, *Emotional Freedom Technique*, or *EFT* as it's known for short, is an extraordinary process which produces almost miraculous results. Similar to Acupuncture or Acupressure, a series of tapping on specific meridian points on the body almost always removes stuck energy. *EFT* can also be used to positively intend what you want to attract.

The theory behind *EFT* is that old negative patterns of emotional response and behaviors get blocked in the body's energy system, stuck in the meridians. By tapping on the meridians while focusing on the problem, the block is removed and the pattern is released.

EFT is an amazingly simple technique for clearing the fears, doubts and limiting beliefs for anything from anxiety and depression to blocks you have concerning money and cash-flow.

For example when it comes to money, *EFT* typically begins with releasing any resistance you have. Most people say they want to get over their money issues, but they don't *believe* they can. They have negative blocks concerning money and many people don't feel worthy and deserving of being financially free. After the negative charge is removed the process can then be repeated to instill positive energy.

To learn how to use EFT and which points to tap, a free manual and several videos are available on Gary Craig's website (www.emofree.com) as well as plenty of articles.

Busting Loose

Busting Loose is a process developed by Robert Scheinfeld (www.bobscheinfeld.com). We have learned, and Bob teaches, that every experience happening to us is *our* creation. Nothing is really *real*. The people in our lives, the words they say and the things they do, are all our creations. Knowing and understanding this is the epitome of taking responsibility for our thoughts!

Since we create this movie called our *'reality'*, we can reclaim the power of our creation by simply reminding ourselves that we created it. Bob has developed an extraordinary, yet simple process to do this called, *Busting Loose*. The results are phenomenal. I strongly urge you to visit his website and experience this for yourself.

Ho'oponopono

Just as extraordinary as the *Busting Loose* process, the *Ho'oponopono* technique was perfected by Dr. Hew Len of Hawaii (www.hooponopono.org).

Ho'oponopono is a process of forgiveness, repentance and transformation. We're taught to take 100% responsibility for our experiences and ask for forgiveness, not from God, but from ourselves.

Everything that appears in our lives is a projection of our beliefs. We have the choice to observe them and let them go, or get caught up in the drama of them. *Ho'oponopono* helps us remember we have this choice. In every moment we have a choice to live our drama or erase the programming and thoughts that create our problems.

The *Ho'oponopono* process is quite simple. Firstly, we must take complete responsibility for our lives. Next, we are taught to say, "I love you. I'm sorry; please forgive me for whatever is going on in my subconscious that is creating this. Thank you."

When we take responsibility like this, we begin the process of forgiveness and transmutation. We are forgiving ourselves and asking that the memories, beliefs and programming are erased.

In order to see results, this cleaning needs to be done all the time. Of course, we will forget and react to something now and again, but the important thing to do is practice this method as much as possible even when it doesn't look like anything is happening. Why? Because these programs are running in the background of our subconscious minds even if we're not aware of it! All of our lives we have reacted to people and situations. When we *erase* instead of *react* we will begin to feel differently, vibrate at a higher frequency and begin to experience inner bliss.

It is important that your positive desires are in harmony with the inner you. If you are not creating what you want, the answer to the problem tends to be inside. Use these tools to clean your 'bowl' before you mix your manifestation recipe.

Getting It

Let's take note of what we learned in this chapter.

- We learned there is a simple recipe for creating what you want; 1. Identify desire, 2. Give attention, 3. Allow.

- To manifest what we want we must be clear of subconscious emotional blocks. It is important to have a clean bowl (mind) to mix our recipe of manifestation.

- Several techniques can be utilized to clean these negative emotional issues such as; hypnosis, meditation, Emotional Freedom Technique (EFT), Scheinfeld's Busting Loose, and Ho'oponopono.

Chapter Fifteen

Living in the Now

We are all *one* energy; God energy, Universal energy, All-That-Is, Source, whatever terminology we want to use, and everything and everyone is connected by being one with this energy. This energy resides in the nothingness called the *Creative Field.*

I've heard the *Creative Field* called; the Void, the Holographic Universe, the Mind of God, Zero Point, and the Super-Conscious Mind. You and I, a tree, the ocean, animals, the planets and stars, the universe, everyone and everything is energy vibrating at a certain frequency.

The *Creative Field* is where manifestation takes place. It is the *substance* used in creation. Since everything is energy and you are energy vibrating, when you create a thought and focus on what you desire, the substance of the *Creative Field* is formed and brought to you. You are truly responsible for creating your reality by your thought. Positive thought (love, joy, happiness, etc.) will bring you a positive reality while the opposite is true for negative thought (worry, fear, resentment, etc.).

Quantum Physics has confirmed that the universe and the world around us is a creation of thought and observation. Our thought is energy and thought-energy creates. All exists in the *Creative Field* and the *Creative Field* is in everything. It is everywhere at once.

There is no *time* as we know it. Everything that is created and experienced takes place in the *'Now'*. Everything already exists. All possible futures exist. Every possible *Now* is in the *Creative Field*. All knowledge, all discoveries to be made, all the wonderful inventions yet to be seen are located in the *Creative Field* and waiting to manifest in the *Now* by our focused thought. How do we do that? By asking for it, placing our attention, energy and focus on it and believing it will happen (allowing).

The Bible tells us we were created in the image and likeness of God. If we substitute the word *energy* for God we can now see the truth in that statement. We were created in the image and likeness of God-energy, and so it follows, we are God-energy in physical bodies. God has been called All-That-Is. *All-That-Is* is energy. Now you understand why we are all *One*; we are *One-Energy*. You can understand that everyone and everything is connected. And since we are *One*, our thought-creations affect everyone and everyone else's thought affects you.

> *We are the creators of our reality. The outer reality we experience is a reflection of our inner reality. If we want a change in the outer reality, change must take place in the inner realty.*

There is no past. There is no future. *Now* is the only time that exists. When you think about the past, when are you thinking about it? Right *now*! When you think about the future, when are you thinking about it? You're thinking about it, and probably worrying about it, right *now*.

Our life is all about *now*, right now at this very moment. Right now and right now and right now, everything is happening right now in the present moment.

Often we look toward our future with thoughts of hope; "When I'm rich I can finally enjoy life." Or, we may look toward the future with frustration; "If things were different I could get a college education and make something of my life." Or maybe our focus is worry; "I better get some health insurance because I could get sick at anytime and hospital bills are astronomical." We're looking towards a future moment that may or may not happen and by focusing there were not living here in the *Now*. This is called *'waiting in the future'* and this is how we give up our power.

Focusing on the past gives away our power too. We may remember a happier time in our lives; "If only I was a kid again. Life was so easy." Or remembering a decision we regret; "I should have waited to get married and have children. Now, my life is a real struggle."

All your hopes for the future and your memories of the past can only happen in the *Now*, the present moment. This is where our power is. *Now* is where we are.

When you are thinking of the past, you are thinking of a *now moment* that happened before *Now*. And, when you're thinking of that former *now moment* you are thinking about it right now. When the future comes to you, it comes to you right now. When you are thinking about the future, you are thinking about it right now.

Are you always looking toward the future or remembering the past so you can feel happy? You can only be happy in the *Now*. If we spend most of our time regretting the past or worrying about the future we place ourselves out of the *Now* where happiness is created.

Our power to create in the *Now* comes from our thoughts and emotions. It's not what happened in the past that keeps us from living an ideal life now. It's holding on to, and focusing on all the drama from our past that will create a similar drama in the *Now*.

You've learned that at every moment you are sending out vibrational energy with your thoughts and feelings. The *Law of Attraction* matches the vibration and gives you more of the same energy. If you send out a thought that you don't have enough money, you will receive more of that vibration; not having enough money.

Starting right now and right now and right now, only send vibrational thoughts that are in alignment with what you want. Don't know what you want? Start with thoughts of gratitude and you will attract more things to be grateful for.

How to Live in the Now

If you have trouble keeping your thoughts in the present moment you have to take control of your mind and not let your mind control you. You see, our minds are conditioned to live in the past and future. This is how we were taught to deal with what we are experiencing in the present.

"Learn for your mistakes." "Remember what happened last time?" Statements like these are programs running in our subconscious and are responsible for your mind escaping the *Now*. Conversely, if your future looks better and gives you hope and anticipation, or it looks bleak and creates worries and fears, your mind has escaped the *Now* as well.

When you deal with everyday problems by escaping to a more joyful time in your past or worrying about or waiting for the future, nothing will change in the *present*, the only place where true happiness occurs.

Are you worried about your future because you're fearful something will happen? Maybe you're concerned you will lose your job, your spouse, or become terminally ill. Ask yourself if any of these problems are happening now. They're not. All your problems are about the future. Is the problem now? No, you're worried about something that isn't happening. It's an illusion.

Are you waiting for things to get better? Maybe you're hoping for success, or a better job or romantic relationship. Waiting is an illusion. It means you are not living in the

Now and using your power to create your future! By living in the *Now*, any situations that arise can be dealt with from the present moment and not from conditioning from your past or anticipation of your future.

Understand there is nothing wrong with setting your vibration for what you want your future to be. We are talking about **Deliberate Manifestation** throughout this book. The important thing to remember is your true power to create the vibrational energy needed to attract what you want must take place in the *Now*.

If your intention is based on your anticipation of the future or from conditioning from the past, you will attract the same conditions again and again. You will always wish it was like it was, hope it gets better, or worry that it won't. Live in the present moment and know you are creating your future at every *now* moment.

Following Your Bliss

Joseph Campbell once said, "Follow your bliss and the universe will open doors for you where there were only walls." True joy and happiness comes from one thing, and one thing only and that is doing what excited us most right now and right now and right now. Doing what makes us most happy at every moment is the only way we will ever experience true joy. How do you know what will bring you joy and happiness? You will know by how you *feel*.

Following your bliss and doing what feels good will be the most beneficial act you can do for yourself and those you come in contact with. When you are overflowing in joy and happiness, you touch everyone with your love and positive vibrations. Can you imagine a world like this?

Unfortunately most of us spend our time doing what we think we need to do rather than what would excite us. How can we be happy waking up in the morning dreading going to a job we hate? The more time we spend doing something we do not enjoy, the more we will try to compensate for that lack of happiness by spending money on things we hope will bring us the joy and happiness we seek. This in turn causes more debt and the need to be tied to a job we hate just to pay the bills and a never ending cycle of pain and disillusionment.

Would you say the majority of people today are caught in this misery? Imagine the negative vibrations this situation has created on this planet. If you put the same amount of energy into following what excites you as you put into the job you hate, you will find joy and hapiness.

I'm not saying to quit your job and spend your days lying in a hammock. That's giving away your power as well. There's a difference in escaping from the life you hate and following your bliss.

Find what truly makes you happy in the present moment and keep following it. If writing a country-western song excites you, do it! If eating a whole chocolate cake gets your blood flowing, do it! How do you find what excites you? You will know by how you *feel*. You will feel free.

Imagine not feeling any guilt, anger, fear, or 'should-have-dones'. That's all from that thing called the past. Feel good, feel happy, feel excitement and this will become that thing called your future… right *Now*!

Follow your bliss and set an example for the other people you come in contact with. People will feel the positive energy you give off and wonder why you are so joyful and happy. Teach them! Show them you're using your mind to deliberately create your reality. Tell them it's their birthright. We were **Born to Manifest**!

- The *Law of Attraction* simply means, I attract to my life whatever I give my attention, energy and focus to, whether good or bad.

- There are two kinds of vibrations, positive and negative.

- The *Law of Attraction* responds to whatever vibration you are sending by matching it and giving you more of it.

- Most people don't realize they can control their thoughts and thereby control the vibrations they send.

- When you talk about what you don't want, you're giving attention to the very thing you don't want and the *Law of Attraction* will give you more.

- When you change your words and go from what you don't want to what you do want, the vibration changes.

- The *Deliberate Attraction* process involves three steps; 1. Identify desire, 2. Give desire attention, and 3. Allowing.

- Briefly observing what you don't want helps get clarity about what you do.

- When you find yourself using negating words like don't, not and no, change your vibration by asking yourself, "What DO I Want?"

- If it feels good, you know you're connected; so do more of it.

- The *Law of Attraction* responds to how you feel.

- Your *Vibrational Aura* holds all the vibrations you're sending out.

- *Allowing* is simply the absence of doubt and limiting beliefs.

- The *Law of Attraction* doesn't know if you're remembering, pretending, celebrating, creating, complaining or worrying. It responds to whatever is held in your *Vibrational Aura*.

- Be thankful. *Gratitude* helps you offer positive vibrations.

- To manifest what we want we must be clear of subconscious emotional blocks. It is important to have a clean bowl (mind) to mix our recipe of manifestation.

- Several techniques can be utilized to clean these negative emotional issues such as; hypnosis, meditation, Emotional Freedom Technique (EFT), Scheinfeld's Busting Loose, and Ho'oponopono.

- Laugh and have fun creating what you want!

Printed in the United States
98463LV00006B/32/A